FALLACIES AND ARGUMENT APPRAISAL

Fallacies and Argument Appraisal presents an introduction to the nature, identification, and causes of fallacious reasoning, along with key questions for evaluation. Drawing from the latest work on fallacies as well as some of the standard ideas that have remained relevant since Aristotle, Christopher W. Tindale investigates central cases of major fallacies in order to understand what has gone wrong and why. Dispensing with the approach that simply assigns labels and brief descriptions, Tindale provides fuller treatments that recognize the dialectical and rhetorical contexts in which fallacies arise.

This volume analyzes major fallacies through accessible, everyday examples. Critical questions are developed for each fallacy to help the student identify them and provide considered evaluations.

Christopher W. Tindale is Professor of Philosophy at the University of Windsor in Canada. He is coeditor of the journal *Informal Logic: Reasoning and Argumentation in Theory and Practice*, author of *Acts of Arguing: A Rhetorical Model of Argument* and *Rhetorical Argumentation*, and coauthor of *Good Reasoning Matters*, third edition.

CRITICAL REASONING AND ARGUMENTATION

General Editors
Douglas Walton, *University of Winnipeg*
Hans V. Hansen, *University of Windsor*

This series is aimed at introductory students in the field of argumentation, informal logic, and critical thinking. Informed by research in linguistics, communication, artificial intelligence, and pragmatics, as well as philosophy, books in this series are up to date in method and presentation, particularly in their emphasis on dialogue and rhetoric, which contrasts with the traditional "go it alone" approach. Each book is designed for use in a one-semester course and includes exercises.

FALLACIES AND
ARGUMENT APPRAISAL

Christopher W. Tindale
University of Windsor

CAMBRIDGE
UNIVERSITY PRESS

CAMBRIDGE
UNIVERSITY PRESS

32 Avenue of the Americas, New York NY 10013-2473, USA

Cambridge University Press is part of the University of Cambridge.

It furthers the University's mission by disseminating knowledge in the pursuit of education, learning and research at the highest international levels of excellence.

www.cambridge.org
Information on this title: www.cambridge.org/9780521603065

© Christopher W. Tindale 2007

First published 2007

A catalogue record for this publication is available from the British Library

Library of Congress Cataloguing in Publication data

Tindale, Christopher W. (Christopher William)
Fallacies and argument appraisal / Christopher W. Tindale.
p.   cm. – (Critical reasoning and argumentation)
Includes bibliographical references and index.
ISBN 0-521-84208-5 (hardback) – ISBN 0-521-60306-4 (pbk.)
1. Fallacies (Logic)   2. Reasoning.   I. Title.   II. Series.
BC175.T56   2007
165–dc22   2006014059

ISBN 978-0-521-84208-2 Hardback
ISBN 978-0-521-60306-5 Paperback

For Jonathan

Contents

Preface   *page* xiii

1 **INTRODUCTION TO THE STUDY OF FALLACIOUSNESS** 1
   1. Strong and Weak Arguments   1
   2. Some Historical Conceptions of Fallacy   6
   3. Approaching Fallacies   12
   4. Why Arguments Go Wrong and How They
       Fool Us   14
   5. Avoiding Fallacious Reasoning   16
   6. Summary   16
   FURTHER READING   17

2 **FALLACIES OF DIVERSION** 19
   1. Straw Man   19
   2. Treatments of the Straw Man   25
   3. Red Herring   28
   4. What Has Gone Wrong in These Examples? Where
       Does the Fallacy Lie?   30
   5. Treatment and Evaluation of the Red Herring   32
   6. Irrelevant Conclusion   34
   CHAPTER EXERCISES   36
   FURTHER READING   40

3 FALLACIES OF STRUCTURE 41
   1. Invalid Structures   41
   2. Fallacies of Distribution   44
   3. Propositional Fallacies   49
   4. Treatments of Propositional Fallacies   50
   5. Formal and Informal Fallacies   52
   CHAPTER EXERCISES   54
   FURTHER READING   55

4 PROBLEMS WITH LANGUAGE 57
   1. Introduction   57
   2. Ambiguity and Equivocation   58
   3. Treatments of the Fallacy of Equivocation   62
   4. Vagueness   64
   5. Treatments of Vagueness   67
   6. Complex Question   69
   7. Treatment of Complex Question   71
   8. Begging the Question   72
   9. Treatments of Begging the Question   75
   CHAPTER EXERCISES   77
   FURTHER READING   80

5 *AD HOMINEM* ARGUMENTS 81
   1. Introduction   81
   2. The General *Ad Hominem*   83
   3. Treatments of *Ad Hominem*   86
   4. Types of *Ad Hominem*   92
   CHAPTER EXERCISES   97
   FURTHER READING   102

6 OTHER *'AD'* ARGUMENTS 104
   1. Introduction   104
   2. *Argumentum Ad Populum*   105
   3. *Argumentum Ad Baculum*   108
   4. *Argumentum Ad Misericordiam*   113
   5. *Argumentum Ad Ignorantiam*   117

6. Summary   121
CHAPTER EXERCISES   121
FURTHER READING   126

7 THE *AD VERECUNDIAM* AND THE MISUSE OF EXPERTS 127
1. Introduction   127
2. Authorities and Experts   128
3. Testimony   130
4. The General Appeal to an Expert   131
5. Ways of Fallaciousness: Complexities of the Appeal   134
6. Summary   143
CHAPTER EXERCISES   144
FURTHER READING   147

8 SAMPLING 149
1. Introduction   149
2. Generalizations   150
3. Treatment of Generalization Fallacies   155
4. Polls and Studies   159
5. Fallacy of Insufficient Statistics   159
6. Fallacy of Biased Statistics   161
7. Measurement Errors   163
CHAPTER EXERCISES   167
FURTHER READING   171

9 CORRELATION AND CAUSE 173
1. Correlations and Causal Reasoning   173
2. The *Post Hoc* Fallacy   174
3. Misidentifying the Cause   179
4. The Argument from Consequences   183
5. The Fallacy of the Slippery Slope   185
6. Distinguishing Causal Slopes from Precedents   188
CHAPTER EXERCISES   189
FURTHER READING   193

10 ANALOGICAL REASONING 194
   1. Principles of Analogy   194
   2. False Analogy   196
   3. Fallacious Appeal to Precedent   201
   4. Two Wrongs by Analogy   205
   CHAPTER EXERCISES   208
   FURTHER READING   213

Index   215

Preface

> The philosophy of reasoning, to be complete, ought to comprise the theory of bad as well as of good reasoning.
>
> — John Stuart Mill, *A System of Logic*

This latest addition to the Cambridge series in Critical Reasoning and Argumentation is a study of bad reasoning, principally as conveyed through traditional and modern fallacies. While the study of fallacies has a long and detailed history, the bulk of critical literature on the fallacies has appeared in the last three or four decades. So much that is new and interesting can be drawn into a full study of the fallacies. The rationale behind this volume is to introduce students to the study of fallacy by means of the latest research in the field, along with some of the standard ideas that have remained relevant since the time of Aristotle. Thus, each topic and fallacy is couched within a discussion of current thinking, providing the clearest explanation possible of both what goes wrong in some of the more prevalent patterns of fallacious reasoning and why arguers and audiences might be misled by such errors.

One thing the recent literature has made very clear is that fallacies are far more complex, and thus deserving of much fuller analyses, than the traditional textbook treatments have suggested. Too often, fallacies are assigned a label and a brief description, along with an admonition to students to avoid such mistakes in their own reasoning. Not only is this insufficient as a treatment of any fallacy, but such an approach also fails to raise the question of how fallacious reasoning might come about in the first place and why it might prove so deceptive. Two things have reinforced the recognition of how complex fallacies really are: The first of these is the appreciation, now fully expressed in the literature, that many of the fallacies are failed instances of good argument schemes or forms. Hence, we cannot dismiss all *ad hominem* arguments or Slippery Slopes, for example, because there are circumstances under which such reasoning is appropriate. What is required, then, is a careful review of the differences between good and bad instances of such schemes. The label/description approach does not allow for this. The second feature that reveals the complexity of fallacious reasoning is the recognition that to evaluate fallacies fully we need to consider aspects of the context in which the argumentation arises. In many instances this involves the details of a dialogue between participants in an argumentative exchange. In other cases we must sift through what is available of the background to a dispute, such as the history of exchanges between the participants or the beliefs of the audience. This brings into consideration dialectical and rhetorical features crucial to understanding and evaluating fallacies and shows that the study involves more than a traditional logical assessment of the propositions involved. It is also important to consider these features when asking how the fallacious reasoning can come about and prove so effective.

Appreciating this complexity further helps explain why we should study the fallacies at all. One response might be that we should simply ignore them, since they demonstrate failures of human reason and do not contribute to our important social debates. But it is because of these things that we are advised to be particularly alert to the presence and nature of fallacies. And if we are to do that, we should give them serious consideration and not relegate them to the status of minor topics touched on in passing. From my own perspective, this recognition has brought about a change of view. Although I was persuaded for a long time that the focus of the study of argumentation should be on good reasoning, the complexity of the fallacies and their interesting rhetorical features have convinced me that a more balanced treatment is important and that, as Mill reminds us, a complete appreciation of argumentation will involve accounts of both good and bad reasoning. The study of fallacies, then, is an important part of a whole approach to argumentation – the more so because it is so revealing of how we actually reason. As with many other activities in which we engage (like reading, writing, or calculation), the norm becomes so commonplace that we fail to notice it and learn from it. It is only when we are confronted with a breakdown of those norms that our attention is caught. In many ways fallacies are breakdowns of the norms of reasoning, and through their study we gain a better understanding of ourselves as reasoners and as members of audiences in social settings.

The approach taken to the fallacies in this book tries to match the seriousness and complexity presented in the foregoing paragraphs. This means in the first instance that I have tried as much as possible to illustrate the fallacies through cases of ordinary reasoning that can arise or have arisen in everyday contexts. We will see less of arguments expressed in just a few lines than of detailed reasoning embedded in larger contexts. The more broad contexts we provide and the more we say about them, the more we may be able to understand what has gone wrong and why. You will certainly find the examples in the exercises at the ends of the later chapters more detailed than some of those earlier in the book. This greater complexity reflects the expected growth of ability and understanding that students should develop as they work through the book. The examples that illustrate fallacies are also presented by means of cases, since cases have a history and a context, involve people, and have consequences. While we will develop principles for dealing with the fallacies studied, any instance or suspected instance of one should be treated as a unique case, assessed on its own terms, since not all ideas associated with a fallacy may apply to any particular case. In this respect, the treatments again reflect what will be encountered outside an academic setting.

Given the conciseness of the book and its introductory nature, some decisions have had to be made about which fallacies to include and which to exclude. In general, I have tried to include the most regularly occurring patterns of fallacious reasoning. A secondary consideration has been given to those that are important historically because of what they illustrate about the nature of fallacies and why people both commit and are deceived by them. The book is designed to work as a companion to Douglas Walton's *Fundamentals of Critical Argumentation*, although it should also work with other good introductions to argumentation or in courses dedicated to the separate study of fallacies. The principal tool used to treat the fallacies is a set of Critical Questions for each. These questions are designed to help the reasoner think through the complexities of a given case, identifying what is at stake and what has gone wrong, and then focusing on the right features to provide a full evaluation.

This book would not have seen the light of day without the encouragement and interest of the late Terry Moore at Cambridge. I hope the final product reflects well as part of his legacy. He will be deeply missed.

My thinking about the fallacies and how they might best be treated has been influenced by a large number of people researching and writing in the field. The debts will be evident in the discussions and references of each chapter. I am particularly indebted to Douglas Walton and Hans V. Hansen for their work as editors of this series and for their own contributions to the understanding of fallacies, the influences of which will be apparent. I have also gained much from recent discussions and written exchanges with Andreas Welzel on the causes of fallacious reasoning and the nature of fallacies as norm violations. During periods of writing over the last few years I have benefited from interactions with a number of students, particularly those at Trent University in my senior seminar on the fallacies. Finally, my former assistant, Daniel Farr, researched many of the examples used in the body of chapters and in exercises. I was indeed fortunate to have had such interested and able help.

CHAPTER 1

Introduction to the Study of Fallaciousness

1 Strong and Weak Arguments

Arguments have a range of types and employ a diversity of devices, from those that press a historical case using causal reasoning to those that recommend an economic course of action by appealing to an authority in the field. They will be characterized by a particular structure, where one or more statements (premises) are given in support of a conclusion, and a range of intentions: to persuade an audience, to resolve a dispute, to achieve agreement in a negotiation, to recommend an action, or to complete an inquiry. Because of these different intentions, arguments arise in different contexts that are part of the argumentative situation. Arguments also have a range of strengths, from those that conform to the principles of good reasoning to those that commit some of the more abysmal errors we will be considering in this book. In between are degrees of strength and weakness. In fact, many arguments of a more extended nature will admit of merits and demerits that can make our judgment about the overall quality of the reasoning quite difficult. A 'fallacy' is a particular kind of egregious error, one that seriously undermines the power of reason in an argument by diverting it or screening it in some way. But a more precise definition is difficult to give and depends on a range of considerations. One famous definition of 'fallacy' that C. L. Hamblin derives from the Aristotelian tradition states: "A fallacious argument, as almost every account from Aristotle onwards tells you, is one that *seems to be valid* but *is not* so."[1] This raises three central questions about the definition: Are fallacies all and only arguments, because Hamblin's definition is strictly speaking a definition of "fallacious argument"? Are fallacies all a matter of validity, which seems to restrict matters to the relations between the parts of an argument? And are fallacies detected through their psychological effect, because if they *seem* valid they must seem so to someone?

To begin addressing these questions and considering the kinds of problematic reasoning that may be elevated (or demoted) to the status of 'fallacy' we will adopt the approach that will be standard in future chapters and explore two cases:

Case 1A

This is from a letter sent to *Scientific American* (January 2, 2002) and it concerns the so-called Lomborg affair, a controversy that erupted in major scientific publications after Bjørn Lomborg published his book *The Skeptical Environmentalist*, in which he challenged many 'orthodoxies' of the environmental movement.

In the 1970s there was a lot of excitement over two books: one theorized that our planet had been visited by friendly aliens who had helped our ancestors with all kinds of "impossible" achievements, including the building of the pyramids; another proposed paranormal explanations for the Bermuda Triangle, complete with "irrefutable" evidence. I can't remember the titles of these books or the authors' names, but I do remember watching one of them being interviewed on television. Although the interviewer was definitely hostile, the author

---

[1] Charles L. Hamblin, *Fallacies* (London: Methuen, 1970), p. 12.

remained confident and self-assured. After 15 minutes or so of well-informed questioning, however, the interviewer had effectively boxed his guest into a corner. At which point the still smiling, recently successful author finally stated, "If I'd said it that way, I probably wouldn't have sold many books."

As far as Lomborg and his book go, I don't think we need look any further than the above statement. Also, growing up and going to school in Cambridge, England, I am extremely disappointed that Lomborg's book was published by Cambridge University Press. I just hope they realize how they have tarnished their reputation by publishing such a work. I think a more suitable vehicle would have been the checkout stand at the local supermarket, which thrives on misinformation and distorted facts.

While the author addresses his comments to the editor of the periodical, his audience will be the general readership. In later chapters we will want to think about the kinds of beliefs and expectations audiences hold and how they may be predisposed to receive or challenge the ideas presented to them. Here we are primarily interested in the position or thesis that the author is promoting and the case he is making for it, because it is in the case that we see a strategy of argument being employed.

Clearly, the writer is antagonistic toward Lomborg's book. He is dismissing its merit as a serious work, judging it rather as a sensationalistic book. He makes this point implicitly rather than explicitly by associating it with two earlier sensationalistic books that made claims about aliens and the Bermuda Triangle. So the case for dismissing Lomborg's work involves associating it with two works that have already been dismissed. They have been judged, we might say, as "guilty" of being nonserious, unscientific work, and the present writer's strategy is to transfer this guilt to Lomborg and his book. Now, sometimes associations do exist and what holds for some partners in an association can be reasonably transferred to others. But we must be given reasons for believing both that an association exists and that a transfer of guilt is relevant. In this argument, no such attempt is made. Thus, the reasoning is weak and the conclusion is not supported. Moreover, in this case we have an identifiable strategy of argument that analysts have judged to be fallacious. The fallacy in question is Guilt by Association. You can see further that the same strategy is employed in the second paragraph. This time the claim is made that Cambridge University Press has tarnished their reputation. But the support for this is the transfer of guilt from the association with Lomborg's book. This time, the association clearly exists, but since the previous guilt was never established, there is nothing to transfer.

Case 1B

This is a letter to the Canadian newspaper *Globe and Mail* (June 19, 2003, p. A16) that contributes to the debate over same-sex marriage in Canada:

The liberal government plans to endorse same-sex marriage based on a lower-court ruling in Ontario (Ottawa Backs Gay Marriage – June 18). Once it does, the well-defined definition of traditional marriage in Canada will be forever altered.

If we allow people to marry without regard to their sex, who is to say that we can't discriminate on the basis of number? It is a small step then to legalizing polygamy.

Once we open up marriage beyond the boundary of one man and one woman only, there will be no difference based on the Charter of Rights and Freedoms between gay marriage and polygamous marriage. Do we want to erode our societal values based on the whims of a small minority? I hope not, and let's not abuse the Charter in this way.

There is much happening in this argument that a full analysis would identify and evaluate, but we are again interested only in the primary strategy the writer employs in opposing this government initiative. The primary reason given for not allowing same-sex couples to marry is that doing so will lead to undesirable consequences because similar cases, here polygamous marriage, would have to be accorded the same right. The writer believes that same-sex marriage will set a precedent for legalizing polygamy. The Appeal to Precedent[2] is another argument form that must meet strict conditions in order to be legitimate. Where such conditions are not met, we would judge the argument again to have the kind of serious weakness that warrants the label 'fallacy'. A precedent is set only if the cases are sufficiently analogous in relevant respects such that what holds for one will hold for the other. One weakness in this argument is that the writer fails to meet a burden of proof to provide the grounds for such analogical reasoning. More specifically, relevant *dissimilarities* between the two cases tell against the belief that legalized polygamy would have to follow. Discrimination on the basis of sexual orientation is a specific concern of the Charter and those involved are recognized as a historically disadvantaged group. No such beliefs or recognition hold for polygamous relationships. More significantly, legislation to permit same-sex marriage is giving gays access to something that everyone else has a right to, a legally recognized "traditional marriage." No advocates of polygamous marriage could insist that they were being denied such rights.

These cases reveal two preliminary things about the evaluation of fallacious arguments. In the first instance, it is not a matter of simply applying a fallacy label to a piece of text and then moving on. What is involved is a careful sifting of claims and meanings against a backdrop of an ongoing debate, and within a wider context. In evaluating the second example, we had to add information to the discussion in order to appreciate the problem involved fully. At the same time, each piece involved the employment of an identifiable strategy. Or, perhaps we should say a misemployment, since

---

[2] This argument is also a candidate for the fallacy called 'Slippery Slope', in which one action is advised against because it will lead (downward) toward other undesirable consequences. The 'Slippery Slope' involves a causal relationship between cases; the 'Appeal to Precedent' involves an analogous relationship between cases. This distinction will be discussed later in the text.

in each case the argumentative strategy could possibly have provided a fitting vehicle to make the writer's point if the appropriate conditions had been met. Hence, as we proceed through our study of various fallacies we will often ask whether they are the countersides of legitimate argument forms, but the appropriate conditions have simply not been met or have been specifically violated. This will force us to be clear about what has gone wrong in each case, and why, and whether the mistake could have been prevented. This also begins to answer one of our earlier questions, that regarding whether fallacies are only arguments. These examples are arguments and, generally, we can see that we are interested in strategies within argumentative discourse. So for our purposes, fallacies will be patterns of reasoning within argumentative discourse, and these will almost always be argument schemes or patterns themselves. A few candidates for fallacies that are not identifiable argument schemes or patterns will arise in the chapters ahead.

2 Some Historical Conceptions of Fallacy

Having this preliminary sense of how we might approach fallacious reasoning has taken us closer to understanding how the term 'fallacy' should be used. To refine this understanding further and to appreciate some of the difficulties that arise when defining and discussing fallacies, we will look briefly at something of the history of this field and the controversies it has engendered.

The story really begins with Aristotle. While there was certainly an appreciation of such mistakes in reasoning earlier, Aristotle was the first to begin categorizing them in a systematic way, first under the title of 'sophistical refutations', in a work of that title, and later with a revised list in the *Rhetoric*.[3] The *Sophistical Refutations*

---

[3] There is also a treatment of fallacy in the *Prior Analytics*, although scholars find no clear doctrine there, nor much that is new. We will take note of this treatment in Chapter 3.

provides a list of thirteen errors. To understand what he meant by a 'sophistical refutation' we need to appreciate something of the dialectical reasoning that was popular with Aristotle and his contemporaries. Many of you may be familiar with Socrates' famous way of proceeding in Plato's *Dialogues*. In search of some important definition, such as the meaning of 'courage' or 'friendship', Socrates would seek out alleged experts who could provide the information required and engage them in discussion. These discussions would have a structure to them whereby a definition or thesis was put forward by the "expert" and Socrates would then ask questions by means of which he gradually demonstrated that the definition failed, or 'refuted' the definition. In Plato's Academy, where Aristotle received his formal training, this model was the basis of a number of structured games or exercises in which one disputant tried to refute the thesis put forward by another. The inquiry would follow certain accepted patterns and be governed by rules. If the right processes were followed, then any resulting refutation would be judged a real one. But Aristotle also recognized that there could be refutations that appeared real but were not so. These he called 'sophistical', thereby associating them with the argumentative practices of the Sophists.[4]

The first six members of the list of thirteen in the *Sophistical Refutations* belong to his classification of refutations that depend on language: Equivocation, Amphiboly, Combination of Words, Division of Words, Accent, and Form of Expression. The remaining refutations are placed in a category that does not depend on language: Accident, *secundum quid*, Consequent, Noncause, Begging the Question, *ignoratio elenchi*, and Many Questions.

---

[4] The Sophists were itinerant teachers in fifth-century Greece. Various doctrines and practices are attributed to them, but the picture is less than clear, in part because of our need to rely on the testimonies of Plato and Aristotle (both firm opponents of the Sophists) for much of our information about them. It does seem, though, that to consider all of their reasoning fallacious would be doing a great injustice to the complexity of their thought.

To illustrate the treatments of this list, we can take as an example the fallacy of Amphiboly, or "double arrangement." As generally interpreted, this fallacy involves an ambiguity arising from the way language is structured. So, a sign in a shop window reading, "Watch repairs here," would seem to qualify as an amphiboly since it is unclear whether the reader is being invited to leave a watch to be repaired, or to observe repairs taking place; hence, the double arrangement. While some modern and contemporary accounts retain this fallacy, it is difficult to find examples of it that arise in arguments and the kinds of ambiguity involved can be covered in a broader treatment of Equivocation.

Aristotle's list in the *Rhetoric* still retains some of the original thirteen, but since his goals were different in that work, other fallacies are introduced. Here he provides nine candidates, all judged "spurious enthymemes" rather than sophistical refutations. A problem may (1) arise from the particular words used; (2) involve an assertion about the whole that is true only of the part, and vice versa; (3) involve the use of indignant language; (4) involve the use of a 'sign', or single instance, as certain evidence; (5) represent the accidental as essential; (6) involve an argument from consequence; (7) involve a false cause; (8) omit mention of time and circumstance; (9) confuse the absolute with the particular. We will see vestiges of some of these in the accounts ahead; others have dropped by the wayside.

As a tradition of fallacy developed out of the Aristotelian account, scholars and teachers have struggled to fit Aristotle's original fallacies into their own discussions. In many instances, such attempts were unsuccessful because the nature of Aristotle's insight arose from the original context of a dialectical debate. Outside such a context, the "fallacy" and its description made little sense. Thus, while contemporary accounts retain some of Aristotle's fallacies, they often take on much different descriptions. Our understanding has simply changed too much for the original description to be completely applicable in modern contexts.

Centuries after Aristotle, C. L. Hamblin reports the sad state of affairs that "we have no *theory* of fallacy at all, in the sense in which we have theories of correct reasoning or inference" (p. 11). Nor do we have any agreement on how a 'fallacy' should be defined. In spite of Hamblin's subsequent claim that "almost every account from Aristotle onwards" identifies a fallacious argument as "one that *seems to be valid* but *is not* so" (p. 12), the weight of recent scholarship would tell against both the claimed tradition and the alleged definition.[5] In short, this standard treatment provides no standard at all. What it does do is emphasize the problems associated with the three central questions that were noted near the start of the chapter.

Hamblin implies that all fallacies are arguments. But some candidates from among Aristotle's original list, such as Accent and Many Questions, are not arguments at all – or, at least, not arguments in the sense that the tradition has tended to give to that term, as a collection of statements, one of which is a conclusion and others of which are premises for it.[6] We have already accounted for this concern in the more expanded working definition for this text, looking at reasoning within argumentative discourse rather than just arguments per se. This will allow us to accommodate Many Questions and other concerns such as Vagueness.

Second, it is asked, are fallacies to be restricted to a failure of validity? Even if this is understood in its widest sense to include both deductive and inductive validity, there remains the stark fact that a traditional fallacy such as the *petito principii*, or Begging the Question (again from Aristotle's list), is not invalid. Hence, we have the strange situation in which Aristotle himself is not committed to the definition ascribed to him. The simplest way for us to respond to this concern in an introductory treatment of fallacies

---

[5] Hans V. Hansen, "The Straw Thing of Fallacy Theory," *Argumentation* 16 (2002), pp. 133–155.

[6] Both qualified, of course, under Aristotle's original concern with dialectical arguments, where what matters are the exchanges that go on in a dialogue.

is to employ a wider criterion than validity. Since a problem such as Begging the Question is a violation of correct procedures even though it is valid, we can speak of fallacies that appear *correct* when they are not.

Perhaps most problematic of all is the final aspect of Hamblin's definition: the *seeming* validity. This vestige of Aristotle's concern between truth and appearance shifts attention from the argument to whoever considers it, whether that be another participant in an argumentative dialogue or a general audience, and deals with its potential to deceive. Many of the examples favoured by textbook authors, and by Aristotle himself, are not particularly deceptive, conveying an obviousness that amuses more than it concerns. This, though, may be more a problem with the examples than the idea behind them. As we look to the importance of contextual features in identifying and assessing many of the fallacies, we will see that this audience-related feature cannot be avoided and so "seeming correctness" will be an important consideration not just in identifying the presence of a fallacy but also explaining how it has come about and why it is effective if it is so.

As befits its dialectical origin, one clear sense of fallacy that we will encounter will involve a shift away from the correct direction in which an argumentative dialogue is progressing. By various means, an arguer may impede the other party from making her point or may attempt to draw the discussion off track. In fact, one popular modern approach to understanding fallacious reasoning is to see it as involving violations of rules that should govern disputes so as to ensure that they are well conducted and resolved. This approach, put forward by van Eemeren and Grootendorst in several works, goes by the name of 'pragma-dialectics'.[7] Not only

---

[7] Frans van Eemeren and Rob Grootendorst, *Speech Acts in Argumentative Discussions* (Dordrecht: Foris, 1984); *Argumentation Communication and Fallacies* (Mahwah, NJ: Erlbaum, 1992); *A Systematic Theory of Argumentation* (Cambridge: Cambridge University Press, 2004).

is each of the traditional fallacies understood as a violation of a discussion rule, but new fallacies emerge to correspond to other violations once we focus on this way of conducting arguments. We find this approach useful in a number of the discussions in future chapters, particularly where there is a clear sense of a dispute that needs to be resolved.

The tradition canvassed by scholars such as Hamblin and Hansen also gives rise to other interesting problems surrounding the nature of fallaciousness, two of which are the following:

The first of these involves the relationship between truth and correctness. For some writers[8] a failure of an argument's premises to be true is sufficient to render that argument fallacious, whereas other authors[9] insist that the correctness or incorrectness of an argument has nothing to do with the truth of the premises. Salmon, for example, writes: "*Logical correctness or incorrectness is completely independent of the truth of the premises.* In particular it is wrong to call an argument 'fallacious' just because it has one or more false premises" (4). To a certain degree, this is a useful move because it avoids the quagmire of deciding what we mean by a premise's 'truth', and in particular, what theory of truth is intended. But it is still a disagreement that warrants attention, particularly considering that the origins of the problem are integral to the way Aristotle identified fallacies with sophistical reasoning. For our purposes, though, we will adopt Salmon's approach and distinguish correctness from truth, concentrating on the former.

The other concern worth noting is one that arose in the beginning of this chapter, the question of whether a form of argument must always be fallacious in order for it to count as a fallacy, or whether fallacies are problematic variants of arguments that

---

[8] Max Black, *Critical Thinking* (Englewood Cliffs, NJ: Prentice-Hall, 1952), pp. 229–230.

[9] Wesley Salmon, *Logic* (Englewood Cliffs, NJ: Prentice-Hall, 1963); James D. Carney and Richard K. Scheer, *Fundamentals of Logic* (New York: Macmillan, 1964).

can have quite legitimate instantiations. The arguments 'ad' are obvious candidates here. While the *ad hominem*, which involves an attack against the person delivering the argument rather than the position argued, was long considered a clear fallacy and all instances of it dismissed as such, more recent work has concluded this not to be the case. There are examples in which an *ad hominem* attack, as a strategy in a court of law or political debate, is perfectly warranted. The challenge to the theorist, as we have already anticipated, then becomes identifying the conditions under which the fallacious instances do arise. Much of our attention in future chapters will be directed to this task.

With respect to this last problem the tradition of fallacies gives us both possibilities. Some cases, such as the *ad hominem* or *ad verecundiam* (Appeal to Authority) can have both legitimate and illegitimate variants depending on whether they meet certain conditions. But not all identified fallacies fit this explanation. A counterexample is the Straw Man or Person. This involves the misrepresentation (deliberate or accidental) of a person's position, a subsequent attack on the misrepresentation, and the conclusion that the person's position has been refuted. There seems no clear way that we can judge this the counterside to some legitimate argumentative strategy, unless we conjure up something trivial such as 'Real Man'. A 'Straw Man' argument would seem to be always incorrect and have no redeemable instances. This means that we cannot define 'fallacy' as the misuse of a legitimate argument strategy because, as with Aristotle's definition, there are recognized fallacies that do not fit. In the chapters that follow, while many of the fallacies we identify will be countersides of legitimate argument schemes, some will have no correct variant.

3 Approaching Fallacies

Because many fallacies are incorrect versions of good argument strategies and because arguments themselves are so embedded in the contexts that create them, identifying and evaluating fallacious reasoning will never be a matter of simply applying a label from a list that can be learned. We will need to consider each case carefully and decide what is involved, whether something has gone wrong, and, if so, what it is that has gone wrong. That is, we need to learn not just how to identify fallacies but also to explain clearly what is fallacious about them. This identification and explanation will then form the basis of a clear and thorough evaluation.

The identification of fallacious arguments is aided by the fact that we are dealing with traditional (and modern) patterns of reasoning that provide specific characteristics in each case. As explained, these patterns will often cover both good and bad instances of an argument type in question; that is, they are value-neutral in terms of the correctness of the argument. Good basic texts in argumentation, such as Douglas Walton's *Fundamentals of Critical Argumentation*,[10] will assist you in recognizing these patterns or schemes, and having this general background before you turn to the study of fallacies will help you. What distinguishes the good from the bad will depend upon whether certain conditions have been met, and that will be our major interest.

To help us consider such conditions and develop our evaluations of specific cases, we will adopt a set of critical questions for each "fallacy," based on what our discussions tell us goes wrong in each case. Armed with these questions, we can then consider a range of arguments in their contexts and evaluate them appropriately.

Our earlier, very preliminary discussion of the fallacy Guilt by Association indicated how there is a specific pattern for the reasoning that will recur in other such cases, and it also demonstrated what it is that goes wrong when the fallacy arises. This will allow us in Chapter 5 to adapt critical questions that we develop for *ad hominem* arguments, where a person's position is dismissed because of his or her character or circumstance (as with his or her

---

[10] Douglas Walton (Cambridge: Cambridge University Press, 2006).

associations). In such instances we will ask, for example, whether the material about the person that is introduced in the premises is relevant to our appraisal of the position or claim, and whether there are grounds for believing the material is factually correct. Our answers to such questions form the core of evaluating fallacies in argument appraisal.

A further feature of our approach in many cases will be raising the question of where the burden of proof lies. This has been an important feature of fallacy analysis since the contributions of Richard Whately (1787–1863). Prior reasoning and understanding will form a presumption in favour of a proposition until sufficient reasons have been stated against it. This is important when we are considering the basic premises in an argument (those that are not themselves supported). Where there is such a presumption in favour of such premises, then the onus or burden of proof lies with anyone who would dispute it. As we will see, one way in which a fallacious move in argument can be made occurs when someone tries to shift the burden of proof onto the other person. As Hamblin (p. 173) points out, we will see this particularly in the case of 'ad' arguments. Indeed, we will see how this works with fallacies such as the *argumentum ad ignorantiam* (appeal to ignorance) or the *argumentum ad populum* (appeal to popularity). It will matter when evaluating the latter, for example, whether the popularity premise has a presumption in its favour or whether the burden of proof lies with the arguer who introduces it.

4   Why Arguments Go Wrong and How They Fool Us

In spite of the best intentions of arguers, some arguments do go wrong. Human reason, as a tool, is not perfect, particularly during the period when we are learning to use it. And since most of us are learning to use it throughout our lives, the opportunities for error never seem to wane. You may not have really thought about this, but you probably have experienced something similar on a physical level. Our bodies are not perfect either, and if we want to improve them, then a lot of hard work is required. Physical excellence comes naturally to few people, and something similar holds for mental excellence. So we should take the study of fallacious reasoning seriously because we can easily fall into such errors if we are not careful.

One obvious occasion when the possibility of fallacious reasoning arises is that when we are closely attached to an issue that is being argued. Full detachment from issues, or complete objectivity, is not possible, so that is not what is being suggested. But we should try to monitor our attachments so that we avoid falling into error. When we feel strongly about a topic we may rush hastily to defend a position, drawing a conclusion that is not fully warranted; or we may not listen carefully to what another person is saying and assume that his position is something it is not; or we may be inclined to engage in personal attacks on the one who holds a contrary view to our own.

Just as we may fall into logical error, so might those around us. None of this is deliberate fallaciousness, and so we should not take deception to be part of the definition of 'fallacy' – at least not as this describes the intent of an arguer. Deception may be an appropriate description of how we come to mistake incorrect arguments for good ones. We have been deceived, not necessarily by the cleverness of an arguer, but perhaps by the closeness in similarity between good and bad arguments of the same form. As Aristotle pointed out back in the *Sophistical Refutations*, people do have a tendency to confuse parts of their experience, and since they see that the ground is wet after it rains, they mistakenly assume that it has rained when they see the ground is wet. This is the kind of error we can all appreciate, and it is not difficult to imagine how such "deceptions" can build into arguments.

Of course, it could also be the case that people do set out to deceive us, that some fallacies are deliberate rather than accidental. If people know what issues we feel strongly about, for example, they may choose to exploit that knowledge by offering arguments that we might quickly adopt although they are fallacious. As we will see in the next chapter, sometimes the misreading of others' arguments in parliamentary debate seems to be a deliberate attempt to sidetrack or derail discussions. But, in spite of these deliberate cases, the fact that fallacies can arise unintentionally shows that deception cannot be part of the definition itself.

5 Avoiding Fallacious Reasoning

It follows from what was said earlier that most of the ways to avoid fallacious reasoning, whether by us or directed at us, reduces to some kind of education. In the earliest textbook on fallacies, if we can call the *Sophistical Refutations* that, Aristotle points to inexperience. Inexperienced people, he tells us, do not get a clear view on things and so confuse the appearance with the reality. And the key way we can overcome such inexperience is by training ourselves to see the counterfeit against the real. This extends from Aristotle's general interest in refutations to the fuller modern-day treatments of argument schemes that have good and bad varieties, according to whether specific conditions have been met.

Learning about these and identifying them as they arise are the first steps in avoiding them ourselves. The next step involves evaluating them fairly and thoroughly. This will give us a further appreciation for why arguments go wrong and how we might correct them.

6 Summary

We start the book, then, with a set of ideas about fallacies and what to expect of them. We also have provisional answers to the three core questions that have been thrown up by the history of fallacies in the Aristotelian tradition.

We are looking not just for arguments but for reasoning within argumentative exchanges, and we do expect the problems involved usually to have a surface correctness about them. So we will not spend much time in the chapters ahead on simple examples that are hardly likely to deceive anyone. On the question of deception, we have seen that no intention to deceive should be part of the definition of 'fallacy'. But that fallacies have the power to undermine reason and deceive us seems clear.

While questions of deductive and inductive validity will specifically interest us in two of the chapters, we will proceed on the understanding that the criterion of interest is correctness rather than validity. This will allow for a wider range of cases to be covered and will avoid the problem that we saw in this chapter.

Furthermore, some fallacies will be counterfeits of good argument forms, thus adding to their deceptiveness. But, again, this cannot be a part of our definition, because other fallacies (as we will see immediately in the next chapter) have no correct form to which to correspond.

We are looking, then, at regular patterns of error that undermine the power of reason in an argumentative exchange (either by shifting attention from where it should be or through some other means yet to be reviewed) but that appear to be correct when they are not. The last phrase directs us to the audience and the context, which we cannot avoid. These things may not play a role in the definition of 'fallacy' but they must be at the heart of its application.

FURTHER READING

Students who are interested in the history of fallacies will find Hamblin's book valuable. Also of value is Frans van Eemeren's chapter "Fallacies" in *Crucial Concepts in Argumentation*, edited by him (Amsterdam: University of Amsterdam Press, 2001), pp. 135–164. A good critical evaluation of Hamblin's tradition is provided by Ralph H. Johnson, *Manifest Rationality* (Mahwah, NJ: Erlbaum, 2000). For modern-day assessments of many of the key fallacies, a good place to start is John Woods and Douglas Walton, *Fallacies: Selected Papers, 1972–1982* (Dordrecht: Foris, 1989).

CHAPTER 2

Fallacies of Diversion

1 Straw Man

For some decades now, argumentation theorists have identified and analysed a fallacious type of argument called the Straw Man fallacy. Although Aristotle makes remarks that suggest a similar concern, the name of the fallacy and its treatment seem modern additions.[1] It is not even mentioned by Hamblin in his seminal work on fallacies.[2] The metaphor captured here reflects a strategy of rebellion or criticism that leads groups of people to build an effigy of a leader (usually with straw) and then attack or burn the effigy, thereby figuratively transferring their "attack" onto the real person. The thinking is that the real person is not available to the group in question and so the effigy serves as a kind of surrogate.

Transferred to the domain of argumentation, this strategy rarely involves any sense of rebellion, but it does retain the tone of a

---

[1] Douglas Walton, "The Straw Man Fallacy," in *Logic and Argumentation*, edited by Johan van Benthem et al. (Amsterdam: Royal Netherlands Academy of Arts & Sciences, 1996), pp. 115–128, attributes the first instance to S. Chase, *Guide to Straight Thinking* (New York: Harper & Row, 1956), p. 40.

[2] Charles L. Hamblin, *Fallacies* (London: Methuen, 1970).

critique and dismissal of whoever or whatever is really at stake. The Straw Man fallacy involves the attribution or assumption of a position, which is then attacked or dismissed. The problem is that the position dismissed by the argument is not the *real* 'man' or 'person', but a caricature of the real position held. In a dialogue, a position may be explicitly attributed to an opponent. But for whatever reason, either that position is not one that the opponent actually holds, or the opponent does not hold the position in quite the way that has been attributed. Hence, an argument that attacks and dismisses the attributed position diverts attention from the real position and is therefore fallacious. Often when there is no direct argumentative exchange between parties an arguer simply assumes that someone who disagrees with her or him holds certain kinds of views. If there are no grounds for that assumption, or the evidence clearly shows it to be wrong, then the argument built on the assumption can be judged a Straw Man.

Consider the following examples:

Case 2A

Politician A: Why is the government once again moving crime to the top of its agenda when far more pressing issues like childhood poverty and environmental devastation continue to be underaddressed?

Politician B: I am surprised that my honorable friend thinks crime is so unimportant. With the alarming increase in gang violence in our cities we face a breakdown of law and order on a major scale. The members of the opposition would wish on us a society in which people could never feel safe even in their own homes.

This is an imagined case, but it is similar to argumentative exchanges that regularly take place in political forums. Politician A is asking the government representative to justify the government's choice of crime as the key issue with which it deals. The rhetorical nature of the question assumes that other issues are more important. But Politician A never states that the issue of crime is unimportant. The government's representative, Politician B, counters with just such a misrepresentation of A's position, attributing that claim to A and proceeding to paint the opposition as a party that does not care about people's safety. Since safety is a concern, the opposition party's "position" must be dismissed. But Politician B has diverted attention from the real question of whether childhood poverty and environmental concerns are more pressing issues and why the government judges crime to be more important. What has been attacked and dismissed is a position that we have no reason to believe A actually holds.

Case 2B

The following is a draft of a bill (HCR74) considered by the Louisiana State Legislature in 2001:[3]

Whereas, the writings of Charles Darwin, the father of evolution, promoted the justification of racism, and his books *On the Origin of Species by Means of Natural Selection: or the Preservation of Favoured Races in the Struggle for Life* and *The Descent of Man* postulate a hierarchy of superior and inferior races. . . .

Therefore, be it resolved that the legislature of Louisiana does hereby deplore all instances and all ideologies of racism, does hereby reject the core concepts of Darwinist ideology that certain races and classes of humans are inherently superior to others, and does hereby condemn the extent to which these philosophies have been used to justify and approve racist practices.

In this case, the proposed bill dismisses Darwinian ideology because its core concepts hold that certain races and classes of humans are inherently superior to others. The conclusion and the reason for it are quite clear. If we can imagine the dialogue that is at stake here, the Darwinism proponent is being dismissed because her or his position is racist. But the portrait painted of Darwinian

---

[3] Reported on *salon.com news*, July 2, 2004.

ideology is a caricature, one not borne out by any objective survey of the works cited. That similar misrepresentations of Darwinian thinking have been used to justify and approve racist practices is beside the point: the position that the legislation is attacking and dismissing is a Straw Man. In subsequent debate this error was recognized, and the eventual bill omitted all mention of Darwin and Darwinist ideology.

We might judge that two things have gone wrong in these examples: (1) an arguer (Politician B or the proponent of the Louisiana bill) has failed to meet an obligation of good argumentation by not ensuring that the position criticized is the actual position held.[4] As arguers we are obligated to treat our opponents fairly, and that fairness includes listening carefully to what they say, knowing their position, and treating it with some respect. In good dialectical exchanges, arguers are also encouraged to consider the strongest point of their opponent's position and try to address that. Deliberately distorting a position by conjuring up a weak caricature of it is not fulfilling that obligation; nor does it do the arguer's own position a lot of good if the strategy is detected.

But the fallacy does not lie in the intent of the arguer to deceive. Straw Man reasoning can arise accidentally as well as deliberately, even if we may tend to give more notice to the intentional strategy. In Case 2A, for example, the misrepresentation would seem to be intentional. Politicians, or individuals in similar kinds of antagonistic relationships that have a certain structure, may come to learn and adopt this strategy of misrepresentation as a matter of course. But one can also misrepresent accidentally, as may have happened in Case 2B. Given that some racist ideology has adopted Darwinian concepts in the past, distorting them to its own ends, we can

---

[4] Douglas Walton, *Fundamentals of Critical Argumentation* (Cambridge: Cambridge University Press, 2006), lists several rules to govern a critical discussion, the third of which reads, "An attack on a viewpoint must represent the viewpoint that has really been advanced by the protagonist" (p. 77).

understand how people concerned about racism could make incorrect assumptions about Darwin's work if they had not reviewed that work themselves. In the heat of debate, we may often think we recognize a position that someone is putting forward, a position for which we have a quick and ready answer, and proceed to attack that position. Reflection may reveal that we have misunderstood what was being said and so our attack was misconceived. The intent may not have been to distort, but the result is still a Straw Man argument, because our argument does not address the real position of our opponent.

(2) Given that the fallacy does not lie in the intention behind it, it must lie elsewhere. This points to the other thing that has gone wrong: the arguer has introduced an *irrelevant* consideration and proceeded to develop an irrelevant argument. Since relevance is an important concept for understanding problems with fallacious reasoning, we need to consider it in some detail here.

Relevance

Relevance must always be understood in argumentation as a *relation*. When it is said that the arguer has introduced an irrelevant consideration, it is appropriate to ask, "Irrelevant to what?" In this case, it is irrelevant to the position that has been stated or that is actually held. One of the conditions governing good arguments is that propositions be relevant to those other propositions they are intended to support. We think of this as *probative relevance* (Walton, 2006, p. 270). In an argument, a relevant premise actively increases or decreases the audience's reasons for holding a conclusion. That is, the premise has a direct bearing on the truth or acceptability of the conclusion. If a premise, even though deemed true or acceptable itself, makes no difference to the conclusion, we say that it is irrelevant to that conclusion. Another condition of good argumentation is that an argument be relevant to its context and background. Broadly speaking, we can capture this under the idea of dialectical relevance.[5] In this case, it must speak directly to that context; however, speaking directly needs to be understood in the context involved. For example, it must answer questions if such are posed, address issues that require a response, and, of course, deal with positions as they were actually understood and intended in the context. Thus, while premise relevance is an internal matter for arguments, we can see that relevance to a context is an external matter.

Some irrelevance is easily detectable because it has nothing to do with what has gone before. We will see examples of this later in the chapter. But fallacious reasoning is often effective because it is subtle and the shifts that take place are hard for the untrained eye to detect. Imagine two portrait artists sketching your portrait. One strives to present something as realistic as possible; the other takes certain key features, perhaps a protruding chin or thick eyelashes, and exaggerates those features to create a humourous caricature. The second portrait still bears some relation to you, since you are the basis for it, but it is not you as you really are nor as you may wish to be presented. Is the second portrait irrelevant to you? This may seem a strange question to ask about portraits, but if we can bear with the example, the answer would be something like "yes and no." It really depends on what will be done with it. In the case of the Straw Man fallacy, the clear irrelevance emerges in the argument that is constructed on the basis of, or in response to, the misrepresentation or caricature. It is important to recognize that *internally*, the argument that is constructed may not exhibit any problems of irrelevance. That is, the relationships between premises and conclusions in the argument are all relevant. The problem is an external one. The argument constructed is irrelevant to the one it should be addressing in the context of

[5] See Walton (2006: chap. 7) for a discussion of this idea.

the debate. Hence, the Straw Man fallacy fails on the second of the two conditions of relevance noted, and it does this whether the misrepresentation was deliberate or unintentional.

2 | Treatments of the Straw Man

Argumentation theorists advise us to avoid debating the distorted version of the position and to check the accuracy of all statements used, and this is good advice. However, what the last revelation about the Straw Man makes clear is that we need to understand this fallacy in relation to the context in which the arguments arise.

The contexts of argumentation are rich and varied. In fact, context is another topic that could occupy us here. Generally, if we want to study fallacies in reasoning seriously and learn how to evaluate them well, we will need to consider different facets of context on different occasions. The context in which argumentation arises can include previous argumentation between the parties involved, previous argumentation on the issue about which we might reasonably expect the parties to be informed, the relationships that might exist between the parties (filial, authority, etc.), commitment sets of those involved, common knowledge about an issue, the time and place at which the argument occurs, the consequences of the outcome of the argumentation for the parties involved, the character of the arguer(s), the composition of the audience (where present), the mode of expression used to convey the argumentation, and so on. This list is not intended to be exhaustive but to illustrate how complex considerations of context can be. When evaluating fallacious arguments we must decide what features of context can be relevant to the specific fallacy involved. Then we can draw these into the Critical Questions we put to an argument to determine whether it does indeed commit a fallacy.

In the case of suspected Straw Man reasoning two Critical Questions will help us to decide whether it has occurred and evaluate the argument accordingly.

Critical Questions

1. Has an opponent's position been misrepresented?
2. Is that misrepresentation the basis for an attack or dismissal of the opponent's claim or argument?

You can see that these questions arise from the definition of the Straw Man fallacy given. In making a charge of Straw Man, the onus is on you to reflect carefully on what is involved in answering these questions and support your findings. Simple yes or no answers will rarely be sufficient since the questions involve some difficult considerations. The first question, for example, raises the issue of how we decide what an arguer's real position actually is. This is particularly challenging in instances such as that in Case 2B where we have no explicit exchange of dialogue from an actual opponent. In those cases, we will often have to draw on our common experience of what is plausible. We tend to be pretty good detectors of exaggeration, so some positions attributed to people will strike us as being particularly implausible. Where someone argues, for example, that we should reject the president's missile defense shield because it will not make North America safe overnight, it seems reasonable to question whether anyone claims or believes that the plan would make North America "safe overnight" and suggest that the arguer is constructing a Straw Man in order to attack the proposal more easily. But subtle exaggerations may be more difficult to detect, particularly if they have some relation to the real position. After all, the caricature of you with the protruding chin or bushy eyebrows is still based on you. Here we have to think carefully about what the actual position is or is likely to be (evaluations based on likelihood will be reasonable in such cases). Features of context that may be of use to us here are the argumentation that is available on the topic in the media and current social or political events that give some clarity or urgency to the issue.

Even where we have an exchange between parties, as in Case 2A, it may still be a challenge to decide what the actual position is and thus whether it has been misrepresented. The key pieces of evidence we have to help us here are the text of the argumentative exchange and any previous argumentation on the issue between the parties or remarks by the person whose position we are trying to determine. This will allow us to make an informed judgment about the commitments of the person, from which we can then extract a consistent position. People are committed to what they say, unless they explicitly state a change of view. In many instances, though, as in the example of Case 2A, a careful review of the statements made in the context will allow us to give a reasonable phrasing of the position and thus decide whether it has been misrepresented by the second party.

The second Critical Question for evaluating potential Straw Man fallacies can also pose some difficulties. The point behind this question is to avoid dismissing an argument as a Straw Man simply because it misquotes someone or exaggerates some aspects of a position but still manages to attack the real position. So the response to the second question depends in part on our success with answering the first. In order to judge whether a misrepresentation is the basis of an attack on a claim or argument, we must first be able to distinguish clearly between the real position and the misrepresentation. Then we can assess the degree to which attention has been diverted away from the real position and the attack has been made against the caricature. Again, simply misquoting someone, while a concern, is not in itself a fallacy. The fallacy arises when the argument constructed in response is irrelevant to the context because it responds to the wrong position.

3 Red Herring

In foxhunting, once the hounds have scent of a fox nothing will deter them from their course except a more powerful scent drawn across the path to lead them off in another direction. A pungent smoked (or red) herring has just such a scent, and these can be used for various reasons to call off a hunt. This metaphor of distraction has been adopted in argumentation to name the fallacy of diverting attention to a new issue so that the other party or audience will completely lose the scent of the original issue. Unlike the Straw Man fallacy, a Red Herring does not involve any misrepresentation of an opponent's position; it is the introduction of another issue altogether, which is not related to the real issue under debate.

Structurally, we may have difficulty determining exactly how the argument of the person committing a Red Herring should be set out because it may not be entirely clear what the person thinks the conclusion is. If the conclusion is the dismissal of the first issue because of what has been said about the second issue, then setting out the components of the argument clearly should quickly bring this problematic strategy to light. This is one way that we will suggest to address the strategy of the Red Herring.

Consider some cases:

Case 2C

The following is a typical argument raised against seal hunts:

Many of your readers seem devastated by the callousness of the annual seal hunt and the culling of seal pups, but their concern is misapplied when they so blithely overlook the real crime being perpetrated every year in this country in the slaughter of thousands of the unborn. Abortion accounts for more deaths of innocents than many wars, but still society does nothing.

The quick response to this may be to allow that they are two very serious issues, but ask how exactly the second is related to the first. The imagined writer is responding to a debate that has obviously developed in the publication's pages over the hunting of seals for their pups. Many people find this offensive and unnecessary. But the writer shifts the focus to a separate issue altogether, one that is not obviously relevant to the first and does not move the discussion back to address the first issue in any way that would contribute to that debate. The difficulty suggests itself, though, in that the writer may well see some connection between the two issues: these are both matters for concern; both issues involve the deaths of 'innocents'. So our judgments regarding the committing of Red Herrings must always involve some consideration of whether there is sufficient relevance of the issues to each other to justify the shift.

Case 2D

This exchange is from the Hansard record of the British Parliament. The debate in question is one that took place just before the invasion of Iraq, in which British forces played a principal role (January 21, 2003, column 156):

Mr. Tam Dalyell (Linlithgow): Which Iraqi opposition groups favour the intense bombing likely to be conducted by the Americans to minimise the number of body bags that will be taken back to Alabama or Wyoming?

Mr. O'Brien: The Iraqi opposition groups want the removal of Saddam Hussein. If there were a choice between a peaceful and democratic regime in Iraq under Saddam Hussein and a war, the issue might be different, but the fact is that Saddam Hussein has carried out the wholesale slaughter of large numbers of his people. I urge my hon.

Friend to remember the 5,000 men, women and children who died at Halabja in 1988 and the 9,000 who were injured there. We need to make sure that Saddam Hussein is recognised as the tyrant that he is, and is dealt with accordingly.

This case illustrates another challenge with recognizing and treating Red Herrings, because Mr. O'Brien's response on behalf of the government does not, strictly speaking, shift to a new issue – he stays with the question of Iraq and the proposed invasion. But does he answer Mr. Dalyell's question? Dalyell complicates matters by posing what we will see in a later chapter to be a Complex Question. That is, if O'Brien were to answer directly, he would run the risk of conceding that the Americans will conduct intense bombing so as to minimize casualties, and he may be reluctant to concede this. But Dalyell's question still demands an answer on whether any Iraqi opposition groups favour intense bombing. O'Brien's response does not address that point at all. Instead, he shifts the focus within the general topic to the crimes of Mr. Hussein's regime and the Iraqi opposition's desire to remove that regime. While related to the topic, the response is not strictly relevant to the question raised and so can be seen to divert attention to ground that is easier to address. In so doing Mr. O'Brien provides a Red Herring.

4   What Has Gone Wrong in These Examples? Where Does the Fallacy Lie?

The key thing that has gone wrong in these examples is that the arguer has shifted the issue to another issue or another aspect of the same issue. As is particularly clear in Case 2D, this strategy may allow the arguer to avoid a difficult question and more easily construct what appears to be a response. The appearance here is important. Where the strategy is successful, it may well be so because people generally agree with the points made: many people do find abortion to be an overlooked issue and even Dalyell may agree with the remarks made about Mr. Hussein and the Iraqi opposition's desire to remove him. But the fallacy lies in the irrelevance of the shift insofar as the initial issue or point is not returned to or addressed. This is again a matter of contextual irrelevance, although in the case of a Red Herring (unlike the Straw Man), setting the argument out in premise and conclusion form may also reveal some internal irrelevance between the premise (dealing with the second issue) and the implied conclusion, which should be saying something about the first issue.

This points to the difficulty noted earlier of actually setting out the writer's argument. Cases such as 2C, for example, will often raise the question of whether the arguer is really advancing an argument or just offering a comment. To determine this we might invoke a Principle of Charity and decide that it would be unfair to attribute an argument to an individual when it is unclear that the person intended the argument and the attributed argument would be clearly fallacious.

Charity is important in fallacy evaluation because it will prevent us from being too hasty in our judgments and force us to consider carefully what was said and what was intended. In a dialogue in which the parties are all present, such as Case 2D, clarifications can be asked for and meanings determined (although the rules governing parliamentary question periods often do not allow for this). But where we have only the text of an argument with no author present we must reconstruct the intended argument as fairly as possible before issuing charges of fallacy. In making such constructions and judgments we would look to draw on features of context already discussed in this chapter, where they are available. Knowing a person's commitments, or what information is likely available to him, will often assist us in deciding what he is likely to have meant. Detecting Red Herring fallacies particularly requires us to employ such caution.

5 Treatment and Evaluation of the Red Herring

When you suspect a Red Herring fallacy has occurred, the following Critical Questions will assist you in confirming the identification and evaluating the argument.

Critical Questions

1. Has the issue been shifted in the course of an argument to another issue or different aspect of the same issue and not shifted back?
2. Is the shift irrelevant to addressing the initial issue?

There are two things to note about these questions that help us to apply them. First, we need to be clear about what the original issue is so that we can judge any shift in the argument. In the more glaring cases of Red Herring this should not be difficult – an arguer jumps from one issue to another one that bears no relation to it. But the more subtle shifts between similar issues or between aspects in an issue will demand attentive reading from you and a judgment on whether a significant shift has taken place.

Second, it is an important condition of the Red Herring that the argument has not been returned to the original issue. The first question requires us to check this for two reasons: in a progressing dialogue it will be natural for one party who thinks another has introduced a Red Herring to demand that the introducer show the relevance of the shift or withdraw it. So our own charge of Red Herring may be premature if the arguer meets the obligation of showing the relevance or withdrawing the point during a subsequent move in the argumentative exchange. Second, we will want to distinguish Red Herrings from another argumentative strategy that will be explored in a later chapter, that is, the strategy of arguing by analogy. In analogical reasoning, an arguer will often introduce a second (or further) issue that she believes is analogous to one under discussion in order to make a point on the basis of the similarities between them. If we do not add to the identification conditions of the Red Herring the clause that it not be taken back to the issue, we run the risk of charging analogical reasoners with the fallacy of Red Herring. As we will see, it is a feature of arguments from analogy that compare issues that the argument is shifted back to the original issue in the conclusion.

After a real shift in issue has been determined, the second question requires us to ask whether that shift is irrelevant to the original issue. This again requires sifting carefully through the context. The philosopher Paul Grice suggested that as communicators we proceed on the assumption that people strive to be relevant. This becomes a key communicative principle. So we should not quickly dismiss a person's shift in an argument without first asking whether there are ways in which the person might think what he has done is relevant, and then judging whether he was correct in that thinking. Of course, if the shift is being deliberately employed as a strategy to distract the opponent from the real issue, then the arguer has no belief in the relevance of the point made. But unless we have good grounds to think that is what is at stake (that is, that the shift was deliberate), then we should give the arguer the benefit of the doubt and look for possible relevant links. This means we look for ways in which the second issue has a direct bearing on what is said about the first. As with the Straw Man judgment, this will take some careful thought and discussion. But as we are discovering, the identification and imputation of fallacious reasoning are not casual or necessarily easy activities. They take time and require that we defend the decisions we arrive at by appealing to the appropriate critical questions.

6 Irrelevant Conclusion

The two fallacies that we have considered so far in this chapter are both major types of diversion, one involving misrepresentation of a position, the other not. The type of irrelevance that we witnessed was contextual in each case. A traditional title for this kind of irrelevance is what has been known as the *ignoratio elenchi* fallacy. This type of failure in reasoning dates back to Aristotle's original list of fallacies, where he uses the label in a general way to mean not proving what one was supposed to prove. In this sense, both the Straw Man and the Red Herring fallacies are types of *ignoratio elenchi*. In fact, even more generally, many fallacies that we will see in subsequent chapters that involve irrelevance in the argumentation can fit under this heading. However, because these fallacies, as do the Straw Man and Red Herring of this chapter, have quite distinctive features that make them irrelevant in their own right, I will treat them as separate fallacies rather than under the *ignoratio elenchi* heading. Instead, I will follow the lead of such logicians as Copi and treat the *ignoratio elenchi* as 'Irrelevant Conclusion'. This often appears as a kind of grab bag label to capture everything not subsumed under the treatments of other fallacies of irrelevance. We will understand it to refer to arguments in which the conclusion "proved" is not the one that was supposed to be proved.

In closing this chapter we will consider briefly a different type of Irrelevant Conclusion in which the irrelevance is internal to an argument. The term often used for the type of irrelevance involved here is *non sequitur*. You will often have reacted to a statement in argumentation by stating, "Hey, that doesn't follow," or heard others raise a similar objection. Here, the concern is that, within the argument, the conclusion does not follow from the premise. Again, many fallacies could be judged as non sequiturs, as we will see. But we want to be able to deal with very general cases of premise irrelevance that do not fall under any other heading, such as the following:

Case 2E

There are more Elvis impersonators in the state of California than students at this institution. Therefore, there is no reason to be concerned about the rise in student numbers.

Quite simply, in this imagined case there seems no obvious connection between what is said in the premise (the first statement) and what is concluded from it, as shown by the 'therefore'. What is important to note is that even if there *are* more Elvis impersonators in the state of California, that makes no difference to our reasons for believing the conclusion stated. What this means is that the truth or acceptability of a premise is a property quite separate from its relevance in a particular context.

Case 2F

This case bears on a controversy that arose when one of Canada's most historic companies, the Hudson's Bay Company, was about to be sold to an American company. Many people thought that because of its historical significance, the company should be protected or remain under Canadian control. In response to this concern one correspondent argued (*Globe and Mail*, August 17, 2004):

Recent letter writers have expressed a great deal of fondness for the historical exploits of Hudson's Bay Co. This company was primarily responsible for manipulating and oppressing the native people, slaughtering millions of helpless animals in the name of fashion and generally being a greed-driven, me-first, ecologically uncaring corporation that worshipped the almighty dollar above all else.

First, we need to assure ourselves that the writer is intending to issue an argument. This may be a case in which the best course is to invoke the Principle of Charity and judge this as an opinion. But that seems inappropriate here because we have a clear disagreement with a point of view that has been previously expressed by others. That point of view was the fondness felt for the historical traditions of the Hudson's Bay Company, given as a reason for retaining it as a Canadian institution. This writer disagrees with that conclusion. So, we do have an argument here. Next, we need to evaluate the relevance of the reasons given to the claim that the Hudson's Bay Company should not be retained. Are the past "crimes" recounted here relevant to the decision of whether to retain the company under Canadian control? This is not as straightforward as Case 2E. Assuming that the writer considers the points to be relevant (that is, invoking Grice's principle of relevance), we need to consider carefully whether there are connections between past misdemeanors and the value of retaining the institution. This example illustrates once again that we must evaluate each case on its own merit and not use fallacy assessment as a simple matter of applying labels and dismissing arguments.

CHAPTER EXERCISES

For each of the following passages, set out the argument so as to identify premises and conclusions and, where it is available, provide a brief statement of the relevant context. Decide whether a fallacy is present and evaluate it by using the appropriate Critical Questions.

1. With stem cell research we stand on the threshold to a future that promises untold benefits in terms of improved health and the elimination of disease. Yet critics tell us we must not go down this path because we do not know what risks may lie there. What kind of attitude is this toward scientific progress? Imagine if the early explorers of space had listened to all the naysayers concerned about

potential risks involved. We would not have reaped the tremendous harvest of knowledge that has resulted.

2. We should be far more concerned about the painkillers we take. In Britain each day aspirin causes enough bleeding to fill three swimming pools.

3. **Reporter:** Mr. Prime Minister, interest rates have almost doubled in the last year. Why is your government doing nothing to help home owners?

   Prime Minister: How can you say we're not helping home owners? I assume home owners eat food, and food prices have fallen for the second time in two months as the result of our policies.

4. Commentators and critics have upped the rhetoric in demanding where are the weapons of mass destruction (WMD) that were supposed to justify the invasion of Iraq. With all the intelligence available, coalition forces would not have gone in without the firm conviction that the WMD could be found, and they will be. What critics forget is that our action has removed a major tyrant from the world stage and freed an entire people who can now work towards democratic self-government. That is something of which we can all be proud.

5. From Hansard UK, March 10, 2003, column 34. Jack Straw was secretary of state for foreign and commonwealth affairs.

   Mr. Robert N. Wareing (Liverpool, West Derby): Will my right hon. Friend explain to the House how the raining of death upon innocent men, women and children can be an acceptable alternative to a policy of containment that is working? Will he listen to the people of this country, who are fed up and tired of him appeasing the United States and the hawks in the White House?

   Mr. Straw: If I thought that there was a viable policy of containment that could work to ensure Saddam's disarmament I would support it, but that is palpably not the case. It is still possible for this matter to be resolved peacefully, but sadly that is Saddam's choice, not ours. With respect, I remember my hon. Friend saying something similar against military action in Kosovo. In the end, that proved necessary and was also right.

6. What the courts must grasp, if they are to resolve justly the debate over assisted suicide in the United States, is that there is no rational, secular basis upon which the government can properly prevent any individual from choosing to end his own life. Rather, it is religious mysticism that energizes the Bush administration into intimidating a doctor who dares to defy their dogma. The conservatives' response to laws that permit assisted suicide stems from the belief that human life is a gift from the Lord, who puts us here on Earth to carry out his will. Thus, the very idea of suicide is anathema, because one who "plays God" by causing his own death, or assisting in the death of another, insults his maker and invites eternal damnation, not to mention divine retribution against the decadent society that permits such sinful behavior. Thus, when religious conservatives use secular laws to enforce their belief in God's will, they threaten the central principle on which America was founded. This principle is freedom of thought, which means freedom from religion.

7. The following is a letter to the *Globe and Mail*, September 6, 2005, commenting on the aftermath of hurricane Katrina's destruction of New Orleans and its surrounding area:

   Regarding your Quote of the Day for Sept. 2, "Philosophers tried to imagine what a 'state of nature' looked like – we're now seeing it inside the United States and it's really brutal." I am hard pressed to find anything remotely natural about thousands of dispossessed people living in a football stadium. It would seem that if a healthy state of nature had been allowed to exist – wetlands and barrier islands left undeveloped and in their natural state – the effects of hurricane Katrina would have been considerably less brutal.

8. From Hansard UK, June 8, 2005, column 1238:

Q2. [1879] Simon Hughes (North Southwark and Bermondsey) (LD):
Will the Prime Minister . . . ensure that British sports policy gives every child in every school a chance to be coached by a professional, so that children have the opportunity and potential to become Olympians themselves one day?

The Prime Minister [Tony Blair]: I fully support the idea of more sport in schools. That is why the Government are making a major investment in school sports co-ordinators, to ensure that kids have the sporting opportunities that they need at school. If we reach our target of four hours of sport a week for children who want it, it will make a great difference – and not just to the health and fitness of the country. I think that sport, including competitive sport, does a great deal for a child's development, and this will be an additional way of achieving more responsible citizenship.

9. From Bernard Hamilton, "Puzzling Success: Specious History, Religious Bigotry and the Power of Symbols in *The Da Vinci Code*," *Times Literary Supplement*, no. 5332, June 10, 2005, 20–21:21. Hamilton is criticizing some of the claims made in the novel. Robert Langdon is the protagonist.

Not merely did the papacy ruthlessly suppress the Knights Templar, it also showed its hatred of the sacred feminine by persecuting witches, but "those deemed 'witches' by the Church included all female scholars, priestesses, gypsies, mystics [and] nature lovers," so Robert Langdon claims. They are all said to be victims of the papal Inquisition, but that is patently untrue, for Protestants persecuted witches with as much zeal and as little discrimination as Catholics did. (There was no papal Inquisition at work in Salem in 1692.)

10. The following is a letter to the *LA Times*, May 24, 2004, accessed May 26, 2004, http://www.latimes.com/news/opinion/letters/la-le-wed24may24,0,5562724.story?coll = la-news-comment-letters:

Re "The Right Can't Win This Fight," by Max Boot, Commentary, May 20: The right must win this fight – for the children. Same-sex marriage suggests that children do not benefit from having a father and a mother.

Death, divorce, abandonment, a single parent's mistakes – any one of these deprives children of a mother or father. But only same-sex marriage would legally ensure that children are deprived from birth of either a mother or a father.

It is dishonest to claim that although children may not be better off, they will be just as well off with two fathers and no mother or two mothers and no father. Does anyone really believe that a mother is useless if a child has two fathers, or that a father is unnecessary if a child has two mothers? Men and women contribute entirely different attributes to rearing children. And, consider the immediate effect on all our children: sex education in school, which begins in the fourth and fifth grades. If same-sex marriage becomes "normal," then our youngsters will have to be taught about same-sex sex. Yikes!

FURTHER READING

Students wishing to study some of the problems raised in this chapter might consult Douglas Walton's *A Pragmatic Theory of Fallacy* (Tuscaloosa: University of Alabama Press, 1995), or his paper "The Straw Man Fallacy" in *Logic and Argumentation*, edited by Johan van Benthem, et al. (Amsterdam: Royal Netherlands Academy of Arts & Sciences, 1996), pp. 115–128. For a fuller account of relevance, see Dan Sperber and Deirdre Wilson, *Relevance: Communication and Cognition* (Cambridge, MA: Harvard University Press, 1986).

CHAPTER 3

Fallacies of Structure

1 Invalid Structures

A key distinction recognized in Chapter 1 had to do with problems that arise within an argument with respect to the support that the premises provide for the conclusion, and also problems that arise "externally," between the argument and its context or audience. The last chapter illustrated both of these problems insofar as the Straw Man, for example, can involve an argument that is internally unproblematic but is fallacious because it is irrelevant to the original position in the context. Similarly, our discussion of *ignoratio elenchi* pointed to the failure of premises to provide any support for the conclusion.

This chapter pursues the last concern by looking at problems that arise with the structure or form of an argument. Here, the argument is presented *as if* the conclusion must follow, given the truth of the premises. But in fact, because of the way terms or propositions within the argument have been organized, the conclusion does not follow from the premises. Traditionally, the claim is that such an argument is invalid, and that invalidity is explained in relation to some particular fallacy. We can see then that one of the traditional features that Hamblin ascribes to Aristotle's definition – its invalidity – is particularly relevant here.

The following is an example of a valid argument, or, to refine our focus, a deductively valid argument:

Case 3A

"The False Promise of Gun Control," *Atlantic Monthly*, March 1994, includes the following argument:

If firearms increase violence and crime, the crime rate should have increased throughout the 1980s, while the national stock of privately owned handguns increased by more than a million units every year of the decade. It did not.

To see the structure of this argument and the conclusion that is being deduced but not stated better, we can set it out as follows:

> If firearms increase violence and crime, the crime rate should have increased throughout the 1980s.
> The crime rate did not increase.
> Therefore, firearms do not increase violence and crime.

This formal pattern of argument bears the traditional name of 'Denying the Consequent'. The first premise sets out a consequent that would follow if a certain condition (the antecedent) were in place. Since the consequent has not followed, we can conclude that the condition was not in place. The argument has an underlying valid pattern or structure. Thus, we can determine one strength of the argument, its validity, merely by looking at this pattern. Assuming the premises are true, the conclusion follows. By the same token, there are traditional patterns that resemble valid ones but that are invalid. Presumably, it is the resemblance that gives rise to the fallacious reasoning: people assume they are considering a valid pattern and miss the fact that it is not. The fallacy associated with Denying the Consequent, which we will consider later in this chapter, has the traditional label 'the Fallacy of Affirming the Consequent'.

Before we proceed to examining some cases of formal fallacies in which the error is due to an incorrect form, there are some preliminary matters to consider. There is an assumption among some logicians that formal fallacies are in better shape than 'informal' fallacies, such as the fallacies of the last chapter and the '*ad*' fallacies, because in formal logic we have clear sets of rules that define validity and invalidity. This assumption has been challenged in the literature[1] on the grounds that while the rules for judging invalidity are clear, the applications of those rules in individual cases and the judgements involved are by no means as straightforward. Massey, for example, is concerned that we can rarely decide that premises are all true and the conclusion false because we are not clear how to prove this. This will be a consideration for discussion at the end of the chapter. For now, it will be sufficient for us to consider arguments that do seem to be fallacious because of formal invalidity.

A further distinction that arises when we explore formal fallacies concerns that between inferences and arguments. The patterns of concern such as the case of Denying the Consequent involve a movement through a chain of reasoning from proposition to proposition. Generally, we call this drawing inferences. An inference may become the conclusion of an argument, but many inferences will not. The underlying structure of formal arguments, however, clearly involves a pattern of inferences, and it is such patterns that we will be exploring. 'Arguments' have further dimensions to them. They have a density of context that gives them a social character. They are part of the ebb and flow of dialogues in the world.

---

[1] See Charles L. Hamblin, *Fallacies* (London: Methuen, 1970); Gerald J. Massey, "Are There Any Good Arguments That Bad Arguments Are Bad?" *Philosophy in Context* 4 (1975), pp. 61–77; and Douglas Walton, *A Pragmatic Theory of Fallacy* (Tuscaloosa: University of Alabama Press, 1995).

Patterns of inferencing can be drawn out of that flux and examined for the relationships between their component parts. But for many argumentation theorists this makes them less interesting and, ultimately, less useful. Still, in terms of our study of 'fallacy' there is something to learn from deductive patterns that succeed and that fail to fit the rules that describe them.

Finally, we should ask whether the invalidity criterion of fallaciousness captured in the idea of arguments that appear valid when they are not relates only to the kind of arguments we are considering here in this chapter. To phrase this another way, will we also wish to speak of nondeductive or inductive validity? If we answer in the negative, then we both restrict the range of arguments to which the traditional definition has application and also leave aside the fact that nondeductive arguments can fail to meet conditions that describe their worth. The problem is contributed to by the fact that it is not always clear that an arguer intends to provide a deductive argument, and so what fails one set of criteria of worth may have merit under another set. This is another reason why we need to look beyond the tradition of formal logic to understand fully the nature of fallacious reasoning.

2 Fallacies of Distribution

One of Aristotle's major contributions to our tradition was the systematic logic captured in his theory of the syllogism. Succinctly put, an Aristotelian syllogism relates terms or categories of things in arguments of three statements: two premises and a conclusion. You will likely be familiar with standard examples such as 'All men are mortal; Socrates is a man; therefore Socrates is mortal'. The three terms of this argument, 'men', 'Socrates', and 'mortal beings', are so related in the three statements that if the premises are true, the conclusion is also true. So this is a valid syllogism. But there are also false or invalid syllogisms. As Aristotle wrote in his

Prior Analytics (II.16.64[b]), "A false syllogism cannot be drawn from true premises," and when this occurs, we have a variety of fallacy.

Aristotle's theory of inference presents syllogism in terms of various figures, or patterns of the three terms, and moods, or patterns of the words that capture the four types of relationship between the terms: 'All', 'No', 'Some', and 'Not all' (or 'Some are not'). The major contribution to our interest in fallacious syllogism was the concept of Distribution introduced in the Middle Ages. A term is said to be 'distributed' in a proposition when it is meant to refer to all members of the class of things that proposition denotes. In the 'Socrates' argument, for example, 'men' is distributed in the first premise, since it refers to all men, while 'mortal beings' is undistributed, since not all mortal beings are captured in the proposition. On the other hand, in 'No politicians are logicians' both 'politicians' and 'logicians' are distributed, since the proposition excludes the entire class of each from the other. 'Some' propositions such as 'Some women are philosophers' have both terms undistributed, since neither the entire class of women nor that of philosophers is being referred to in the proposition. Finally, a 'Not all' proposition such as 'Not all fallacies are easy to detect' is equivalent to the proposition 'Some fallacies are not things that are easy to detect'. Here 'fallacies' is undistributed because only some of them are denoted. But they are being excluded from the entire class of things that are easy to detect, so that class is distributed. What we have seen about Distribution can be captured in the following table:

All S (distributed) are P (undistributed).
No S (distributed) is P (distributed).
Some S (undistributed) is P (undistributed).
Some S (undistributed) is not P (distributed).

The rules of validity for syllogisms put forward by logicians developed over time and contain requirements that govern the number of terms and propositions involved. For our purposes, we can focus on the rules for Distribution and look at the three modified rules that Hamblin (p. 199) considers provide us with a "satisfactory modern theory":

1. The middle term must be distributed at least once.
2. No term must be distributed in the conclusion that was not distributed in the premise in which it arose.
3. There can only be one negative premise, and if there is, there must also be a negative conclusion.[2]

Consider an argument that violates rule 1:

Case 3B

All people with conservative values support the war. Some religious leaders support the war. So, some religious leaders must have conservative values.

We can see that this argument meets the conditions of having three propositions, two premises and a conclusion, and three terms, 'people with conservative values', 'supporters of the war', and 'religious leaders'. Thus identified, the argument can be set out as follows:

Premise: All people with conservative values are supporters of the war.

Premise: Some religious leaders are supporters of the war.

Conclusion: Some religious leaders are people with conservative values.[3]

Rule 1 tells us the middle term must be distributed at least once. The middle term in a syllogism is the term that the two premises

---

[2] Rule 3 does not refer to 'Distribution' but depends on the concept.

[3] You may feel that the conclusion is a true proposition. But our interest is whether it can be concluded from the two premises that are supposed to prove it.

have in common. In this case, the middle term is 'supporters of the war'. A valid syllogism shows the relationship of two terms in the conclusion by virtue of the relationship each has with a 'middle' term in the two premises. If the middle term is not distributed at least once, such that the entire class is referred to, then it is possible that the other terms are being related to a different portion of the middle term, in which case no conclusion can be drawn about the relationship between those other two terms (in this case, between religious leaders and people with conservative values).

The argument we are evaluating has the following Distribution pattern:

Premise: All people with conservative values (distributed) are supporters of the war (undistributed).
Premise: Some religious leaders (undistributed) are supporters of the war (undistributed).
Conclusion: Some religious leaders (undistributed) are people with conservative values (undistributed).

The middle term, 'supporters of the war', is undistributed in both premises, so this argument has an invalid structure. We can say it commits the Fallacy of the Undistributed Middle.

The second rule can be violated when either of the terms in the conclusion is distributed but had not been distributed in the premise in which it arose. This means that the conclusion contains more information than the premises warrant, or, put another way, we are drawing a conclusion about all of a class denoted by the term based on information about only a portion of that class. The next case illustrates this problem.

Case 3C

All Westerners are overconsumers. But no Japanese are Westerners. Therefore, no Japanese are overconsumers.

Again, we have three propositions and three terms or classes of things. This argument can be set out to show the following Distribution pattern:

Premise: All Westerners (distributed) are overconsumers (undistributed).

Premise: No Japanese (distributed) are Westerners (distributed).

Conclusion: No Japanese (distributed) are overconsumers (distributed).

We have two terms in the conclusion, 'Japanese' and 'overconsumers'. The first of these is distributed in both the conclusion and the second premise. But 'overconsumers' is distributed in the conclusion but not in the first premise. Since this is called the major premise, the term in it besides the middle term is called the major term. The fallacy we have identified here is the Fallacy of the Illicit Major. If the same problem had been with the term in the second, minor, premise and the conclusion, then we would have a Fallacy of the Illicit Minor.

Finally, the following argument violates the third of our earlier rules.

Case 3D

No Third World countries are free from the AIDS epidemic. And not all Third World countries have economies that can afford the cost of drugs needed to fight the AIDS epidemic. So, not all Third World countries that have economies that can afford the cost of drugs needed to fight the AIDS epidemic are free from the AIDS epidemic.

The problem with this argument is that each of the propositions excludes classes from each other. On this basis, no conclusion can be drawn about any relationship between the classes. The fallacy involved we shall call, following Hamblin (p. 200), the Fallacy of Negativity. As we will see later, one of the reasons someone might be confused by this argument is a tendency to read into the second premise the proposition 'Some Third World countries *are* countries that have economies that can afford the cost of drugs needed to fight the AIDS epidemic'. Such a reading needs to be resisted because the premise, as given, clearly is a denial of the 'all' generalization, and where the 'all' is false, the 'some are not' proposition must be true.[4]

3 | Propositional Fallacies

Just as arguments that involve relationships between terms or classes can have fallacious variants, so too can arguments that express relationships between types of proposition. We will look at two such cases, exploring the second in more detail. If we know that one thing follows from another, it is easy to imagine that it will not arise if the first is not present. But to reason so is to commit a fallacy called 'Denying the Antecedent'.

Case 3E

If the people believe the government is honest, then the government will win another term in office. But the people don't believe the government is honest, so they will not win a further term.

The problem here is that the first premise is assumed to issue a necessary condition, without which the consequence could not follow, when all it may really offer is a sufficient condition: enough to bring about the consequent, but not necessary for it, since other conditions might also bring it about. Strictly speaking, then, the first premise only tells us what would follow *if* a certain antecedent arose. It tells us nothing about what would happen

---

[4] No complete review of syllogistic fallacies has been attempted here. That would involve a further discussion of whether the terms involved are empty, or fail to have members.

without that antecedent. Hence, the conclusion need not follow from the premises, and the argument is fallacious as a result of this structure.

While the titles and discussions of these problems arise later in the tradition, Aristotle recognized the basic tendency to error when he observed in the *Sophistical Refutations* that if one thing follows from another, it is easy for us to imagine it the other way around, to convert the relationship. "If B follows from A we imagine A must follow from B." This pattern of erroneous inference we now call 'Affirming the Consequent'. Aristotle provided several examples of what is at stake, including the following:

Case 3F
> If it has rained, the ground is wet.
> The ground is wet.
> Therefore it has rained.

In fact, the first premise provides us with a condition by which we can infer what is the case *if* the antecedent holds true and is affirmed in the second premise. But we have no grounds to draw a conclusion if the Consequent is affirmed in the second premise. Other things besides rain could account for the wetness of the ground. Aristotle makes this clear in further accounting for this mistake: "Because every man in a fever is hot, it does not follow that every man who is hot is in a fever." But we can see how easy it might be to confuse the relationship between antecedent and consequent and how important it is to be clear about which relationship has been expressed.

4   Treatments of Propositional Fallacies

Aristotle's explanation for how such formal fallacies can arise is a useful one. It is clear that if we have one form that is valid and another that is very similar to it but invalid, then someone could confuse the two. That is why formal fallacies are sometimes called fallacies of resemblance. Walton (p. 73) takes this explanation further in stressing that what the false reasoner (or someone duped by such reasoning) does is take as a necessary condition for bringing something about a condition that is only sufficient. A necessary condition for X is a condition that must be in place in every instance for X to occur. Thus, if we have X, we can reason back to the presence of the condition. A sufficient condition is one that could bring about X, but is not necessary for X to occur; other conditions could also exist that would be sufficient to account for X. Rain, for example, is sufficient to account for the wetness of the ground, but so too would be a spill of some fluid, or an underground water source seeping to the surface.

Thus, if we want to suggest some Critical Questions to assist in the recognition and appraisal of formal fallacies, we would need to go further than proposing questions that only checked for the occurrence of invalid forms. For the earlier fallacies of syllogism we could offer questions such as the following:

Critical Questions

1. Does the argument have three propositions involving relationships among three and only three terms?
2. Have the rules of Distribution been obeyed such that the conclusion must follow from the premises?

The first question allows us to identify the argument as one appropriate to the analysis we are providing, and the second applies the key concern with Distribution.[5] The focus here is on the

---

[5] As Hamblin (p. 201) points out, while these rules allow us to identify individual cases of fallacious argument, given that any argument may violate more than one of the rules, there is no strict correspondence between rules and fallacies such that we can derive a clear classification of fallacies.

Distribution of the terms within the argument rather than the rote learning of the pattern.

Similarly, for the propositional arguments we have reviewed, we can ask other questions:

Critical Questions

1. Does the argument involve a relationship between propositions such that the intent is for the conclusion to follow from the premises?
2. Have the expressed relationships between the antecedent and consequent been correctly identified so that there is no treatment of a merely sufficient condition as if it were necessary?

Here, the second question takes us beyond just recognizing the underlying form as invalid, because it allows that in some circumstances (where a necessary condition is involved), the conversion of consequent and antecedent is appropriate. This means that some cases of the patterns we have identified will not be fallacious.

5   Formal and Informal Fallacies

This last point brings more clearly to light the concern expressed at the start of the chapter. While we may assume that the state of formal fallacies is in better theoretical repair than that of the informal cousins, matters are not quite so straightforward. We cannot, for example, just dismiss arguments because of their patterns but must look carefully at what they *say*. So formal fallacies are not just a matter of form, and the apparent gap between them and informal fallacies begins to close. The common denominator in the case of both is the underlying context that must be understood and explored before a clear attribution of fallacy can be made.

In this light, it is perhaps not surprising that Aristotle identified the problem with consequent that we saw earlier not so much as a formal fallacy but with what he calls "rhetorical argument." A proof by signs, for example, may be based on consequences, whereby a man is "proved" to be an adulterer because he exhibits the characteristics (or signs) of an adulterer by dressing elaborately or wandering at night. While the signs may be true, the accusation is false. Deciding the quality of such arguments requires us to go beyond the form to its meanings and our experience in general. We must explore them in their natural language setting.

Lessons from the history of formal fallacies confirm this advice. One traditional fallacy associated with the syllogism, for example, is the 'Fallacy of Four Terms'. By definition, a syllogism has three and only three terms (each appearing twice). Sometimes it may look as if there are three terms, but when we actually explore the meanings involved we recognize that there are four. How might this happen in a situation in which people may be plausibly misled into believing there were three terms when there were in fact four? The likely cases are ones in which a term is ambiguous, that is, reference is made to more than one of its meanings. But where this occurs, we are no longer looking strictly at the underlying form, and the fallacy involved is that of Equivocation (see the next chapter), which is identified by considering the argument in its natural language setting.

Likewise, it seems that while every argument that has the form of a valid argument is also valid, as confusing as it might sound, not every argument that has the form of an invalid argument is an invalid argument. There are instances of the form 'Affirming the Consequent', for example, that are not fallacious in which there is one and only one condition that would bring about a state of affairs.

Suspected fallacious cases, then, need to be considered very carefully in their natural setting, and not simply extracted from their contexts to be tested for validity. On these terms, our general approach differs not at all from the way we approach other fallacies in this book. While logicians may continue to debate such questions as whether the valid/invalid distinction can be extended to cover inductive arguments, it may be more useful to use a distinction such as strong/weak to cover all arguments and allow that validity and invalidity, where they can be determined, are part of the overall assessments of strength and weakness.

CHAPTER EXERCISES

Use the rules and Critical Questions of this chapter to evaluate the following examples and determine which ones involve fallacious reasoning. With cases of 'Affirming the Consequent', decide whether there is only one condition that could bring about the conclusion.

1. If Woody is a New Yorker, then he's an American. Woody is an American. Thus, he's a New Yorker.

2. "Science and Technology," *Economist*, July 21, 1990, p. 85:

    If optical fibres were perfect, they would lose no signal; because they are not, signals being sent over long distances have to be amplified at regular instances.

3. All New Yorkers are American. Woody is an American. Therefore, Woody is a New Yorker.

4. If modern environmental pollutants were responsible for certain cancers, we would have seen a rise in instances of those cancers over the past three decades. And we have seen a rise of those cancers over that period. This confirms that modern environmental pollutants were the culprit.

5. The Iraq strategy was ill judged, the execution was inept, and it may end up hastening the relative decline of American power. But it must be seen as primarily an attempt to ensure America's future strategic dominance, if the alternative is to believe that Dick Cheney, Donald Rumsfeld, and Condoleezza Rice are frivolous people who do not act in accord with their own understanding of the strategic situation – an alternative that is not plausible.

6. Cloning technology is so new that it is not covered by the law of the land. Anything outside the law of the land is illegal. So, cloning technology is illegal.

7. None of the seafood is fit to be eaten because it has been allowed to spoil and most foods that are allowed to spoil are not fit to be eaten.

8. If the body is dead, then there are no vital signs. There are no vital signs. Thus, the body is dead.

9. **Simon:** I wish I didn't have to do these exercises because there's no point to them.

   Susan: On the contrary, there is a point to them because they will help develop your mind.

   Simon: So?

   Susan: So, anything that helps develop your mind is worthwhile.

10. If this book is full of fallacies, then its conclusions cannot be trusted. Unfortunately, it is full of fallacies.

FURTHER READING

A deeper appreciation of some of the issues in this chapter, and particularly the relationship between informal and formal fallacies, can be found in the paper by Massey ("Are There Any

Good Arguments That Bad Arguments Are Bad?" *Philosophy in Context* 4 [1975], pp. 61–77), and in Chapter 3 of Douglas Walton's *A Pragmatic Theory of Fallacy* (Tuscaloosa: University of Alabama Press, 1995). For a discussion of formal theories in informal logic see Chapter 17 in John Woods and Douglas Walton's *Fallacies: Selected Papers 1972–1982* (Dordrecht: Foris, 1989).

CHAPTER 4

Problems with Language

1 Introduction

As we saw in Chapter 1, Aristotle divided fallacies into those that depended on language and those that did not. Since then among fallacy theorists this has been a popular approach to the organization of fallacies. Until recently, many theorists even repeated the fallacies of language that Aristotle had identified, even where these made little contemporary sense. More recently, we have seen the list expanded to include "new" fallacies of language that reflect modern usage and experience.

On the question of which problems of language are fallacies we also encounter some of the deeper issues of what is to count as a fallacy. Some traditional fallacies of language are not arguments, for example, and some that are do not seem to be invalid. Both these points will be discussed in relation to fallacies taken up in this chapter.

Aristotle's list of fallacies that depend on language numbered six: Equivocation, Amphiboly, Combination of Words, Division of Words, Accent, and Form of Expression. The first two of these can still be found in contemporary lists in the way that Aristotle understood them. We will return to these later. The other four, where they have been retained, have undergone considerable revision of meaning. Aristotle's combination of words and division of words differ considerably from their contemporary instantiations as the fallacies of composition and division. Aristotle was concerned with the ways in which combining and dividing words alter meanings. As he writes: "A man can walk when sitting or write when not writing. The meaning is different as 'sitting' is conjoined with 'can' or with 'walk'"(*Sophistical Refutations* 166a). So, we have 'a man *can* walk when sitting' or 'a man can walk-sitting'. In distinction, modern-day accounts of composition treat the fallacy as one dependent not on language but on the parts and wholes of extralinguistic objects.[1] Thus, we see examples like 'each part of the machine is light; therefore the machine is light'.

Aristotle's fallacy of Accent has even less contemporary relevance. Because Greek is an accented language, meanings could shift depending on how a word was accented through rises and drops of intonation or the pronunciation of long or short vowels. In nonaccented languages, the problem disappears. It persists in contemporary accounts only insofar as theorists are able to distort it to cover change of emphasis on various words in a sentence. But this is not what Aristotle had in mind, particularly when it is changed to include any kind of emphasis,[2] and likewise with Form of Expression (or Figure of Speech), which involves being misled by the structure or root of a word. Modern writers who include this have difficulty finding plausible examples.

2 Ambiguity and Equivocation

The remaining two, Equivocation and Amphiboly, involve ambiguity. In the case of Amphiboly, this ambiguity arises from the

---

[1] Hans V. Hansen and Robert C. Pinto, *Fallacies: Classical and Contemporary Readings* (University Park, PA: Penn State University Press, 1995), p. 5.
[2] Charles L. Hamblin, *Fallacies* (London: Methuen, 1970), p. 25.

sentence structure. The words used are unambiguous in themselves, but when put together in a statement they create an ambiguity. So we see such examples as 'apartment available for man with small toilet'. Many puns in sitcoms depend on this kind of humorous ambiguity. The problem for the student of fallacies is to know how seriously to take such instances. Modern textbooks seem unable to provide examples that have much import, and we would of course not consider examples like the one preceding as arguments. Nor do they appear particularly deceptive; they arise more from carelessness and error. For our purposes, we will observe only the sense of multiple meanings that make such cases ambiguous and use this appreciation for the next type of example.

This brings us to the one fallacy of language from Aristotle's list that does deserve serious study: Equivocation. Ambiguity can arise in arguments in a number of ways. We may have a word or concept that has more than one potential meaning in a given context. Hence, it is ambiguous. In most cases, the context itself will tell us which of the potential meanings is most likely to have been intended. Again, an entire phrase or statement can be similarly ambiguous until we resolve the ambiguity through consideration of the context. While these kinds of ambiguity are clearly problems with language that can impede communication and even mislead, they are not obviously fallacious, if we restrict ourselves to the argument condition for fallacies. Equivocation, however, involves the shifting of meaning of a term, concept, or phrase within the process of an argument. Hence, arguments that equivocate in this way are fallacious arguments. For example, although a term may be introduced with one meaning, over the course of the argument another meaning of the same term is introduced or assumed.

Consider the following case:

Case 4A

This is part of a discussion from Plato's dialogue *Euthydemus* (298E):

[**Dionysodorus**]: Ctesippus, just tell me this, have you a dog?
  Yes, a real rogue, said Ctesippus.
  Has he got puppies?
  Yes, a set of rogues like him.
  Then is the dog their father?
  Yes, indeed; I saw him with my own eyes covering the bitch.
  Well now, is not the dog yours?
  Certainly, he said.
  Thus he is a father, and yours, and accordingly the dog turns out to be your father, and you a brother of whelps.

This is a classic case of Equivocation, from one of the earliest accounts dealing with fallacies. Yet many people have had trouble deciding exactly what goes wrong here. Succinctly put, Dionysodorus's argument is 'You have a dog, the dog is a father, and therefore the dog is your father'. For our purposes, we can appreciate that something can 'be yours' in a wide range of senses, from your idea to your turn to your place in history. The meaning of one sense cannot be transferred to another. This is what Dionysodorus's argument purports to do, from 'your dog' to 'your father'. Once we appreciate that we do not possess a dog in the way we have a father, the nature of the fallacy emerges.

Note here that the equivocation of the term is committed by the same participant in the argumentative dialogue. That is, the one who first introduces the term and its meaning is the same person who subsequently shifts the meaning. If we have two arguers who are simply assuming different senses of a term, concept, or phrase, we would not say that either of them has committed a fallacy of Equivocation. Instead, we would judge that they had engaged in a dispute that was really verbal rather than real, since once the ambiguity was resolved it may transpire that they do not actually disagree. Or, it may be that the second arguer has constructed a Straw Man by attributing a meaning to the first arguer that he or she did not intend.

This next argument shows the subtlety involved with this fallacy.

Case 4B

The following is adapted from a debate on the relationship between aging drivers and dementia:

Your claims about an increase of aging drivers with dementia fan the flames against older motorists. The big risk, so you claim, is the coming multitude of drivers with dementia unleashed on the highway. You give the impression of a multitude of safe, younger drivers inundated by a growing minority of demented seniors at the wheel. The risk is worse because the signs of dementia "are so subtle." Anyone driving in a major city today does not have to look hard to find signs of demented drivers, but few of these are aged, and the indications are not so subtle. We have young and middle-aged (rarely old) drivers chatting obliviously on cellphones as they perilously negotiate crowded streets at hazardous speeds, we have the mid-30s executive in his/her SUV charging through red lights, we even have the youthful bicycle courier risking his life – and that of others – on the road.

There is a lot going on in this argument beyond what interests us in this chapter, but the core of what is being argued is that the major risk on the roads is not from demented older drivers because few of today's demented drivers are aged. We can see what has gone wrong here because the conclusion is being drawn about the term 'demented' in one sense, whereas the supporting premises involved that term in a different sense. As the term 'dementia' (or 'demented') is used to refer to older people it means an illness; but as it applies to irresponsible drivers (of all ages) it refers to craziness. The difference is between being in a certain state and acting as if one were in a similar state. The arguer's position is that we face more danger from people who act in crazy ways. But what is said fails to address the relevant question because of the equivocation.

Once again, we could judge the fallacy here to be the general one of irrelevance (*ignoratio elenchi*) because the argument does not prove what it was supposed to prove, that older drivers are not so demented or dangerous. But as with other distinctly identifiable fallacies, this one has its own conditions that reflect what has gone wrong. By focusing on the matter of Equivocation, we can see how such a fallacy can mislead an audience and seem to be correct. After all, the arguer appears to be talking about the same thing throughout and stays on the topic of safe driving. It is only by close attention to the terms used and their different senses that we catch the shift that has occurred.

3   Treatments of the Fallacy of Equivocation

Treatments of Equivocation vary, but all appreciate it as a serious fallacy because of its potential to mislead. It has even been argued that Equivocation is the *only* fallacy because all fallacious reasoning hinges on ambiguity of some variety.[3] Agreement exists, though, that using a term, concept, or phrase *as if* its meaning had stayed the same when in fact it has been shifted from one sense to another is fallacious and potentially deceptive. Doing so can frustrate the resolution of a dispute[4] and exploits the audience that does not carefully review the meanings of all terms used but trusts an arguer to stay with the usages first introduced. Given the wealth of senses that most words possess, it is not difficult to see how people can succumb to this fallacy, especially in the subtler cases. The following Critical Questions will help us decide whether a

---

[3] See, for example, Lawrence H. Powers, "Equivocation," in Hansen and Pinto, *Fallacies*, pp. 287–301. Powers, however, understands fallacies to depend on the argument and appearance conditions. So a case of, for example, the Fallacy of Affirming the Consequent in the previous chapter is on his terms an invalid argument, but not a fallacy.

[4] Fran van Eemeren and Rob Grootendorst, *Argumentation, Communication, and Fallacies: A Pragma-Dialectical Perspective* (Mahwah, NJ: Erlbaum, 1992), p. 202.

fallacy of equivocation has been committed and to analyze suspected examples.

Critical Questions

1. Have key terms, concepts, or phrases retained their initial meanings throughout the argument?
2. Does any shift of meaning indicate that the conclusion fails to prove what it was supposed to prove?

It is a condition for the fallacy of Equivocation to occur that one or more terms, concepts, or phrases within an argument have a shift in meaning. So where we suspect this has occurred, we will need to justify our judgment by identifying the offending items and clearly stating the different senses of the term, concept, or phrase involved. Since Equivocation can arise as a result of the haste or oversight of an arguer, it will not be a matter of determining the meaning that was *intended*. Instead, we are looking at objective usages of the term, concept, or phrase. That is, as with 'demented' in 4B, there are objective and accepted meanings that terms have, and it is these meanings that a community of language users shares in common and thus expects. If an arguer explicitly defines a term in a certain way, then we still need to be sure that she then uses the term consistently throughout the argument. When arguers fail to do this, they equivocate, whether they intended to or not.

The second Critical Question is required because a shift in meaning, while necessary for the fallacy of Equivocation to occur, is not enough. That shift must result in the conclusion's failure to follow from the premises. Thus, it is possible for the argument to appear to be correct, but not to be so. Equivocation can occur within an argument without the emergence of the full problem. We could have a term equivocated on in the premises, for example.

While this is a problem, it is not the serious problem that arises when the fallacy occurs. Problems in premises can be remedied, or there may still be sufficient unproblematic premises to support the conclusion. But where the premises assume one sense of a term, concept, or phrase and the conclusion is drawn about that term, concept, or phrase in a different sense, then there is a breakdown between premises and conclusion that cannot be remedied. When an arguer equivocates in this way, he or she has committed a fallacy.

4 Vagueness

Is there a fallacy of Vagueness? Theorists disagree on the answer to this question and part of that disagreement hinges on how we understand fallacies. Vagueness obscures the meanings of terms or phrases so that people cannot be sure what accepting statements would commit them to, or how to evaluate such statements. Many writers simply treat vagueness as a problem with terms or phrases in an argument that prevents the audience or antagonist from understanding what is being said. Others treat it as a full-fledged fallacy. Van Eemeren and Grootendorst (1992), for example, suggest that if a participant in a critical discussion makes use of unclearness to improve his position, then he is guilty of violating one of the dialectical rules that govern critical discussions. Such a violation they call the fallacy of unclearness. We need to consider carefully how someone could improve her position through introducing vagueness, because one of the problems with vagueness is that it cannot be controlled. That is, terms or phrases are vague when one cannot determine what they mean in a given context. Where this is the case, there is a danger that an antagonist or audience will assign their own meanings, thus taking control from the arguer. Hence, the use of vagueness would not seem to be a good strategy for improving one's position in a discussion.

Another popular approach[5] identifies a Fallacy of Vagueness in arguments, where it is hard to determine what the argument is. Again, this presents difficulties: it would seem that on such an understanding, vagueness should be not so much a type of argument as an impediment to engaging in argument. A problem here is that we cannot be sure someone intended to argue if we cannot determine what the argument is. We have the strange circumstance suggested of (1) knowing there *is* an argument **and** (2) not knowing what the argument is (other than that it is vague). We might wonder that if (2) is the case, how can we be sure of (1)? Let us consider some potential cases:

Case 4C

In his well-known essay "Politics and the English Language,"[6] George Orwell rails against imprecision of all types. One of his examples to illustrate his complaint is taken from Professor Harold Laski (essay in *Freedom of Expression*):

I am not, indeed, sure whether it is not true to say that the Milton who once seemed not unlike a seventeenth-century Shelley had not become, out of an experience ever more bitter in each year, more alien [*sic*] to the founder of that Jesuit sect which nothing could induce him to tolerate.

As Orwell notes, Laski uses five negatives in fifty-three words, along with some avoidable clumsiness, thus rendering the passage meaningless. We really do not know what Laski is trying to say. Of course, if this is the case, then we also cannot be sure whether he

---

[5] Ralph Johnson and J. Anthony Blair's (1993) account of the Fallacy of Vagueness centres on two conditions: first, "an argument contains a premise, or a conclusion, whose meaning is indeterminate"; second, "the indeterminateness of this statement makes it impossible to assess its acceptability as a premise or its significance as a conclusion." *Logical Self-Defense*, 3rd ed. (Toronto: McGraw-Hill Ryerson, 1993), p. 153.

[6] George Orwell, "Politics and the English Language," *Horizon* 13 (1946), pp. 252–265.

was trying to present an argument. The context might help us, but Orwell provides none of it. Clearly, Laski has committed a serious error of communication. But has he committed a fallacy? We can determine neither whether Laski has improved his own position in some debate, nor whether his discourse contains premises and conclusion.

Case 4D

This case is from the results of one of the bad writing contests run by the journal *Philosophy and Literature* (1998). The example originates in the *Australasian Journal of American Studies* (December 1997) and is entitled "Museum Pieces: Politics and Knowledge at the American Museum of Natural History":

Natural history museums, like the American Museum, constitute one decisive means for power to de-privatize and re-publicize, if only ever so slightly, the realms of death by putting dead remains into public service as social tokens of collective life, rereading dead fossils as chronicles of life's everlasting quest for survival, and canonizing now dead individuals as nomological emblems of still living collectives in Nature and History. An anatomo-politics of human and non-human bodies is sustained by accumulating and classifying such necroliths in the museum's observational/expositional performances.

This piece could be explaining what natural history museums do or can do. But if what is claimed about them in this way is not obvious (and it is not), then it could alternatively be arguing that this is what they can do, with a supporting premise in the last sentence. If so, this would fit the kind of scenario that Johnson and Blair envisage, in which we have an argument, but we do not know what it is. That 'not-knowing' arises from the obscurity of some of the words used ('nomological', 'anatomo-politics', 'necroliths'), along with combinations of words giving rise to unclear ideas ('dead remains ... as social tokens of collective life'). In other words, the whole thing is vague. And one suspects, for the reasons just given, that the context from which it was taken would not readily help us to resolve the vagueness.

Vagueness is the first instance of a clear problem in which we must decide whether something has to be an argument in order to be a fallacy. After all, cases like 4D could be dealt with by invoking the Principle of Charity that was discussed in Chapter 2, because if we really do not know what the argument is, what is gained by attributing an argument to an author? Furthermore, if we insist that a fallacy in order to exist must *seem* to be correct, then vagueness is difficult to include. Vague passages seem to be nothing but vague; if an audience takes them to have a certain meaning, then they are not vague.

At the same time, there clearly is a problem here, one that could well impede us from dealing well with arguments, and we want to be able to handle such cases.

5 Treatments of Vagueness

It makes most sense in light of the foregoing discussion for us to treat vagueness as a problem that impedes us from engaging in arguments because where it arises we cannot be sure whether an argument is intended or what it would be. As such, we can use the following Critical Questions to deal with suspected cases.

Critical Questions

1. Does a word, concept, or phrase have no clear meaning in the context in which it arises?
2. Does that vagueness prevent us from being able to judge whether an argument has occurred or what it might be?

The first question is important for identification because it distinguishes the problem involved from that of ambiguity, which infected the fallacy of Equivocation. Ambiguity occurs when we have more than one plausible sense that can be attributed to a word, concept, or phrase in a context. By contrast, something is vague when there is *no* plausible sense to attribute to it. It is not a matter of having too many meanings, but of having none at all. But crucial to deciding whether Vagueness has occurred is the second idea in this first question, that of context. As this was first introduced and discussed in Chapter 2, context involves a number of features, many of which can be helpful in resolving potential vagueness. We need to look carefully at any previous stages in the dialogue between the arguers to see whether there are meanings there that shed light on what has been said later. Or, if available, other discourse from the same arguer might be examined to see whether a term, concept, or phrase has been defined by her elsewhere. In a similar way, we can review the "environment" of the debate or argument. What else has been going on that provides a context for what is said? What issues might we expect the participants to be familiar with and even drawing on for their statements? In Case 4D, for example, an ongoing discussion in society about the role of natural history museums could form the backdrop for the statements whose meaning we are trying to ascertain. If nothing in the available context can help us resolve the potential vagueness, then we have to judge it as actual and move to the second Critical Question.

For vagueness to be a problem for us it must have the specific consequence of impeding argumentation, by obscuring either its presence or its components. If terms are vague, but we can still clearly see the argument, then no fallacy has occurred. As we saw in the discussion of Case 4D, charity is called for here: we do not want to attribute to someone a position he never intended. But arguers also have an obligation to use language that is clear and accessible to the audience they are addressing. Where we cannot decide what it is we are being asked to accept and commit to, or even whether we are being asked to commit to anything, then the writer or speaker has failed in this primary obligation. Communication has been prevented, agreement is not possible, and any disputation is at an impasse.

6 | Complex Question

The problem called 'Complex Question' is another fallacy candidate. Although it seems appropriate to consider it under fallacies of language, Aristotle included it in his list of those that did *not* have this dependency. It is similar to Vagueness in that it is also a matter of debate as to whether this should be treated as a fallacy because it is not an argument. It is different from Vagueness, and so useful for our ongoing analysis, because it introduces the issue of assumptions.

Its questionable status as an argument is suggested by the very label assigned to it. Questions are not declarative statements that can be judged true or false and accepted or rejected. Questions require a different kind of response than statements. For this reason, few theorists are inclined to include 'Complex Question' in any stable of fallacies. The variant of this problem, Many Questions, was the last fallacy in Aristotle's list, but even on Aristotle's treatment, the fallacy label seems inaccurate.[7]

A Complex Question is not a straightforward one: it contains an assumption that is hidden but that must be implicitly acknowledged if the respondent is to answer the question. Invariably, such an acknowledgement commits the respondent to a position or claim with which she is at least uncomfortable, and to which she may be adamantly opposed. Since it contains such an assumption, a Complex Question can be unpacked to reveal two or more statements and thus could be revealed to have the structure of a simple argument. Consider the following example.

[7] Hamblin, *Fallacies*, p. 4.

Case 4E

When are you going to wake up to what's going on?

To answer this question, a respondent must implicitly concede that he has not been alert to what is going on. It can be unpacked to read:

> Since you have been unaware of what's going on, you need to wake up to it.

Cast this way, it is not really a question at all but an accusation. Answering this seems to force the respondent to concede that the accusation is correct.

To see how this strategy might work in real life, consider the following exchange between the British MP Robert Wareing and Foreign Secretary Jack Straw (Hansard UK, March 10, 2003: column 34):

Case 4F

Mr. Robert N. Wareing (Liverpool, West Derby): Will my right hon. Friend explain to the House how the raining of death upon innocent men, women and children can be an acceptable alternative to a policy of containment that is working? Will he listen to the people of this country, who are fed up and tired of him appeasing the United States and the hawks in the White House?

Mr. Straw: If I thought that there was a viable policy of containment that could work to ensure Saddam's disarmament I would support it, but that is palpably not the case. It is still possible for this matter to be resolved peacefully, but sadly that is Saddam's choice, not ours. With respect, I remember my hon. Friend saying something similar against military action in Kosovo. In the end, that proved necessary and was also right.

When we looked at this case in an earlier chapter, we focused on the reply. This time, notice how Wareing's two questions have been structured to contain assumptions that Straw is sure to find unpalatable and have difficulty answering. A direct response to the first question, for example, would have to accept both the 'raining of death' description and the presumption that the current policy of containment was working.

7 Treatment of Complex Question

Whether or not we take Complex Question as a fallacy, it introduces us to the problem of unacceptable assumptions that can be hidden by statements or questions. Complex Questions are the problems they are because they cannot be answered without the respondent's being committed in some way to the assumptions contained in them. Even questions that require just a yes/no response like the old saw "Have you stopped beating your dog (or robbing banks, or engaging in public nudity)?" presuppose that the respondent *has* been beating his dog, and so on. Some examples will involve assumptions that, once drawn out, constitute full arguments. But whether or not this is the case, all instances of Complex Question are problematic for the reasons shown and we need to consider how to deal with them.

Critical Questions

1. Does the question contain hidden assumptions that commit the respondent to some unacceptable situation?
2. Would answering the question directly involve an unfair shift of the burden of proof in the argumentative exchange?

As with past fallacies, the first question is an identification question. On the terms we have discussed here, a question is a complex one if it contains assumptions that commit the respondent in some way. So the first task in our analysis is to identify the assumptions involved, as we did in Case 4F. The challenge here is to identify assumptions correctly, since these are hidden. All statements involve some assumptions (even if it is just a basic assumption that the audience understands what is meant), but some of these can be controversial. A statement such as "I wish the government would stop pandering to special interest groups" clearly assumes that the government *is* pandering in this way. In argumentation, the proponent of such a statement has a burden of proof to support the assumptions involved. By hiding them in this way the person can sometimes illegitimately avoid the burden of proof. This is what is happening with Complex Questions. So our task is to identify the assumptions and show why they would be controversial in the context. That is, we must show how they commit the respondent to something that is unacceptable.

The second question addresses what is wrong with such a strategy. Simply put, Complex Questions require responses that are unfair to the respondent and give the asker an advantage. The burden should lie with the questioner to justify the assumption, but the burden has been shifted to the respondent, who must defend herself against what is only an implication. The respondent might then appear guilty because she has in some way conceded the assumption simply by responding to it. More important, a fallacy has been committed because of the unfair shift in the burden of proof. The questioner has an obligation to support assumptions but has not done so.

8 Begging the Question

Circular reasoning that is deemed to be fallacious is said to 'beg the question'. Traditionally, this has been called the fallacy of *petitio principii* and you will still see references to the *petitio*. When told that an argument begs the question, it is appropriate for someone to wonder what question is being begged, because invariably with circular arguments there is no actual question being asked. Instead, the "question" in question is the issue that is being discussed or the claim being argued. This fallacy is linked to the problem in the section Complex Question in that here the key concern is also one of *assumption*. Someone begs the question when she assumes in the premises the very thing she is asserting in the conclusion. Since the same statement cannot be used to prove itself, the argument is circular. In recent vernacular it has become popular to say someone begs the question simply when he *raises* an issue. That is not the traditional meaning of the phrase and not the way we are using it here.

Begging the Question is a fallacy that deeply concerned Aristotle. In the *Sophistical Refutations*, it arises in the list of fallacies that are independent of language because the fallacy depends on assuming the original conclusion. But there is also a modern interest that concerns the meanings of propositions and that idea is related to one of Aristotle's senses. In his *Topics* (162b 34), he speaks of its occurring in five ways:

People appear to beg their original question in five ways: the first and most obvious being if any one begs the actual point requiring to be shown: this is easily detected when put in so many words; but it is more apt to escape detection in the case of different terms, or a term and an expression, that mean the same thing. A second way occurs whenever any one begs universally something which he has to demonstrate in a particular case: suppose (e.g.) he were trying to prove that the knowledge of contraries is one and were to claim that the knowledge of opposites in general is one: for then he is generally thought to be begging, along with a number of other things, that which he ought to have shown by itself. A third way is if any one were to beg in particular cases what he undertakes to show universally: e.g. if he undertook to show that the knowledge of contraries is always one, and begged it of certain pairs of contraries: for he also is generally considered to be begging independently and by itself what, together with a number of other things, he ought to have shown. Again, a man begs the question if he begs his conclusion piecemeal: supposing e.g. that he had to show that medicine is a science of what leads to health and to disease, and were to claim first the one, then the other; or, fifthly, if he were to beg the one or the other of a pair of statements that necessarily involve one another; e.g. if he had to show that the diagonal is incommensurable with the side, and were to beg that the side is incommensurable with the diagonal.

Not all of these seem relevant to modern concerns, particularly the fourth and fifth.[8] Woods and Walton[9] (1989) follow several earlier commentators in focusing on two variants of Begging the Question that capture the core of Aristotle's account: those that express 'equivalence' and those that express 'dependency'. In the limited space that we have here, adopting this twofold approach will more than meet our needs. In the first sense, an argument begs the question because the conclusion is effectively equivalent in wording or meaning to a premise on which it depends for support (Aristotle's first way). In the second sense, the conclusion and premise have a relationship of dependency such that in order to accept one we must already accept the other (the underlying sense of the second to fifth ways).

Let us look at an example of each of these two senses:

Case 4G

A heavier-than-air craft could never fly because in order to lift up and travel over distance a machine would have to be lighter than the environs surrounding it.

As Aristotle points out, the first sense of Begging the Question is easily detected when people just use the same thing to support itself, but detection can fail when different terms or expressions that have the same meaning are involved. That is what has happened in this case. When we look closely at the meanings of the

---

[8] John Woods, *Paradox and Consistency: Conflict Resolution in the Abstract Sciences* (Cambridge: Cambridge University Press, 2003), p. 26.

[9] John Woods and Douglas Walton, *Fallacies: Selected Papers 1972–1982* (Dordrecht: Foris, 1989).

words in the claim and in the premise (what follows 'because') we can see that they amount to the same thing but are worded in a different way. A 'heavier-than-air craft' is a 'machine...lighter than the environs surrounding it'; 'flying' involves lifting up and traveling over a distance. Closely scrutinized, the premise is not a reason for the claim, since it simply repeats what is said there.

Case 4H

God is the only perfect being and perfection includes all the virtues. So, we know that God is benevolent.

Here the problem of circularity lies not so much in the language chosen but in the assumptions being made. Aristotle's second way of Begging the Question involves trying to prove something by using ideas that already assume the truth of what it is you are trying to prove. In this case, if God has all the virtues, then the premise is already assuming that God has the virtue of benevolence, which is the very thing to be proved.

9 Treatments of Begging the Question

Case 4H introduces the complexity that has led to so much discussion of this fallacy, and even the question of whether it is a fallacy. You will recall from Chapter 1 that one criterion of fallaciousness is that something appears valid when it is not. The problem here is that circular arguments are valid arguments. So cases like Begging the Question challenge us to rethink the nature of a fallacy. Generally, we can argue that the arguments are still fallacious because they do not offer an independent reason for the claim they are trying to support (hence the 'dependency' problem).

Another important insight about Begging the Question, which emerges from the reference to a 'question', is that this is a problem that arises in dialogues. Mill[10] recognizes this in observing that no one is likely to commit this error in her own reflections. But in the context of a dialogue, when asked to support a point, she may well try to support something by supposing proved what she has yet to prove. Similarly, Hamblin (p. 33) traces the origins of the fallacy to Greek dialogues of disputation, when one person asks another to grant a certain premise on which to build a point, but then proceeds to act as if the granted premise has actually been proved. Both of these insights can help us construct our Critical Questions of identification and evaluation:

Critical Questions

1. Has the arguer avoided the obligation to provide independent support for a claim by restating it in similar terms?
2. Has an arguer avoided the obligation to provide independent support by assuming somewhere in the premises the very thing that has to be shown?

The reference to an obligation in the first question identifies the dialectical situations in which this fallacy most plausibly arises. As Mill noted, it is when challenged that we may assume more than our reasoning warrants. In making such an assumption, we fail to meet the basic obligation we take on as arguers to provide independent support for contested or questionable claims. The need to evaluate terms for their similarity of meaning stresses why we should still treat this as a fallacy of language rather than assign it, as Aristotle did, to the other basic category. A tendency to repeat terms or expressions should alert us to the potential presence of circularity. But we need also ensure that we do not mistake repetition for circularity. Repeating a term or expression for emphasis

---

[10] John Stuart Mill, *A System of Logic* (London: Longmans, Green, 1900), Bk. V, chap. VII.

is a perfectly acceptable and often rhetorically powerful strategy. It need not involve circularity at all if we are not asked to accept something on the basis of its reiteration. Hence, the fallacy occurs only when the repetition is being advanced as support for itself in some other form.

In directing us from the language itself to what is being assumed, the second Critical Question requires us again to attend carefully to the context. In dialogues, we can take note of what is being granted for the sake of argument, and then watch that no shift takes place so that what has been granted this way is treated as if it had actually been proved. Admittedly, it can be a more difficult task to detect when the second sense of the fallacy occurs and a premise already assumes the truth of the very claim it is supposed to support. We can address this concern by asking of each premise the grounds on which we, or its audience, are being asked to accept it. Perhaps it is on the basis of a prior argument, or common experience. Asking this question will expose cases in which we discover that the grounds by which we should accept a premise is the very point that we are supposed to see being proved in the conclusion. Where we can show this to occur, we have detected an instance of the fallacy of Begging the Question.

CHAPTER EXERCISES

Evaluate each of the following passages for fallacious reasoning, using the Critical Questions and discussions of this chapter to aid your identifications and justification.

1. **A:** Our company can offer you the best price for the job and reliable service.

    B: How can I be sure of that?

    A: Well, C across town will vouch for our reliability.

B: And why should I trust C?

A: Well, I can assure you that C is reliable and can be trusted.

2. Capitalism is the best form of government because it alone governs in a way that is agreeable to the interests of most people.

3. Addressing journalists in Brussels, Belgium, U.S. Defense Secretary Donald Rumsfeld on the state of U.S. intelligence regarding terrorist threats, "Rumsfeld baffles press with 'known unknowns,'" ABC News Online, June 7, 2002:

There are things we know that we know. There are known unknowns – that is to say, there are things that we know we don't know – but there are also unknown unknowns. There are things we do not know we don't know. So when we do the best we can and we pull all this information together, and we say well that's basically what we see as the situation, there is really only the known knowns and the known unknowns. And each year we discover a few more of those unknown unknowns.

4. From Plato's dialogue *Euthydemus*:

[Dionysodorus]: You tell me you wish [Cleinias] to become wise?

[Socrates]: Certainly.
     And at present, he asked, is Cleinias wise or not?
     He says he is not yet so – he is no vain pretender.
     And you, he went on, wish him to become wise, and not to be ignorant?
     We agreed.
     So you wish him to become what he is not, and to be no longer what he now is. . . . Of course then, since you wish him to be no longer what he now is, you wish him, apparently, to be dead.

5. The world is made of matter and matter is eternal; therefore the world is eternal and cannot have been created.

6. People who scream so loudly about 'sanctity of life' in opposing abortions should think twice about their position when these same

individuals fervently support the execution of criminals by the state.

7. **A:** People always act in such a way as to promote their own interests.

   B: What about someone like Mother Teresa? She clearly seems to be a person who acted selflessly in putting others' interests first.

   A: If she wasn't interested in acting that way, she wouldn't have done so. So this just serves to support my point.

8. From a letter to the *Belfast Telegraph*, May 20, 2004, accessed May 31, 2004, http://www.belfasttelegraph.co.uk/news/letters/story.jsp?story=523132:

   CONTRARY to the claims of the Belfast Telegraph's editorial (May 17), the Republic's smoking in public places ban must not come north. I am one of many people who cannot agree to such a move.

   If Government was to ban smoking in our own homes, then there would, quite rightly, be uproar. It wouldn't take a Sherlock Holmes investigation to find out why that might be: Government has no business making such a law with respect to private property.

   The problem with all the fuzzy thinking lately (exemplified in the Telegraph's leader), is the failure to recognise that most pubs and restaurants are not public places.

   They are, like many houses – privately owned. Why then shouldn't the owner of the pub or restaurant decide, just like the owner of a house decides, whether his private property is smoking or non-smoking? And subsequently, people can decide whether or not they want to visit.

9. Accessed June 2, 2004, http://www.fsmitha.com/com/philosophies.htm#science:

   Some people complain that science is not based on certainty. They believe in certainty and that their own view of reality is built upon certainties.

   Scientists, on the other hand, build on the approximations – the approximations of their predecessors. They are supposed to recognize that they are imperfect and to subject their ideas to criticism. And some scientists look forward to their approximations being improved upon in the future.

Some who see their beliefs as drawn from certainties – from absolute truth – give little credence to the need of people to weigh and interpret. They see truth as Plato saw it – as inborn. They dismiss their own need to interpret as unnecessary, or they see questioning as blasphemous.

Some who believe in certainty claim to be opposed to relativism, yet, in dismissing the need to weigh and interpret they leave people free of any standard for belief. For example, they have nothing to offer to rival Osama bin Laden's dogmatism or the point of view of anyone else, including someone who claims to have killed because he heard God's voice tell him to kill.

FURTHER READING

A number of the works mentioned in the notes for this chapter will provide deeper explorations of some of the concerns with fallacies and language. In particular, Lawrence Powers's article on equivocation and several of the chapters in the Woods and Walton collection are recommended for further reading. In addition to these, readers interested in exploring these matters further should consult Douglas Walton's *Fallacies Arising from Ambiguity* (Dordrecht: Kluwer Publishing, 1996).

CHAPTER 5

Ad Hominem Arguments

1 Introduction

In the wide public domain, where controversial issues are debated and personalities invariably clash, the strategy of attacking an opponent because of some real or perceived characteristic, circumstance, or association is particularly prevalent. The strategy of attacking the person falls under the general umbrella of ethotic arguments, that is, arguments that deal with some feature of the character of the speaker.[1] Where the attack is problematic in particular ways, we charge the attacker with committing the fallacy called *argumentum ad hominem* (argument against the person). We have to be clear that we are speaking here of the *fallacy* involved in this strategy. While the textbook tradition for a long time treated all such arguments as fallacious, more recent treatments have appreciated that it is often quite appropriate to draw attention to some feature of a person's character or circumstances when it

---

[1] We can trace the general category back to Aristotle in his *Rhetoric*, where he observes that the character of whoever presents an argument is often instrumental in the acceptance of that argument.

has a direct bearing on what that person says. Part of the previous confusion was due to the extreme looseness of many textbook treatments of this fallacy. There is also the further complication that the way the *ad hominem* has been understood and treated over time has changed. We need to consider some of this history and then fix on what modern treatments identify as problematic.

The first philosopher to draw attention to the *ad hominem* is John Locke (1632–1704), although he does not claim to have invented the term, and Hamblin[2] attributes the idea, if not the title, to Aristotle. Here, not surprisingly, it arises in the context of dialogues. In the *Sophistical Refutations* (177b33), Aristotle writes with reference to an example, "this solution will not suit every argument . . . but is directed against the questioner, not against the argument." This is in fact closer to the modern sense than what Locke subsequently introduced, since it clearly identifies the problem as a shift from a person's argument to the person. Locke introduces it as one of four types of argument (we will see two others later) that people may use to persuade others or at least silence their opposition. Here, the arguing is "to press a man with consequences drawn from his principles or concessions."[3] In Locke's mind, then, the *ad hominem* is a matter of self-consistency, and while he does not explicitly identify it as a fallacy, other things he says indicates that it may well have fallacious occurrences depending on the appropriateness of the charge.

We have here two versions of what may be at stake with a fallacious *argumentum ad hominem*. One involves some kind of shift from the person's argument to the person and the other involves showing the person to be inconsistent in some way. As we will see, the complexity of modern treatments of the *ad hominem* allows us to accommodate both concerns.

---

[2] Charles L. Hamblin, *Fallacies* (London: Methuen, 1970), p. 161.
[3] John Locke, *An Essay Concerning Human Understanding*, edited by A. C. Fraser (New York: Dover, 1959 [1690]), sect. 21.

2 The General *Ad Hominem*

Case 5A

The first example we will consider is drawn from a case introduced in Chapter 1 concerning the publication in 2001 by Bjørn Lomborg, a statistician and political scientist at the University of Aarhus in Denmark, of the book *The Skeptical Environmentalist*. There quickly arose a heated debate between Lomborg and his defenders and members of the scientific establishment. Because he is not himself an expert in the field of environmental science or any of its cognate disciplines, his expertise has often been challenged. More questionably, his youth and status as "only" an assistant professor have also been used to undermine his credibility. The following is from a long critique in *Scientific American* (January 2002), p. 62:

And who is Lomborg, I wondered, and why haven't I come across him at any of the meetings where the usual suspects debate costs, benefits, extinction rates, carrying capacity or cloud feedback? I couldn't recall reading any scientific or policy contributions from him either. But there was this massive 515-page tome with a whopping 2,930 endnotes to wade through. On page xx of his preface, Lomborg admits, "I am not myself an expert as regards environmental problems" – truer words are not found in the rest of the book, as I'll soon illustrate. I will report primarily on the thick global warming chapter and its 600-plus endnotes. That kind of deadweight of detail alone conjures at least the trappings of comprehensive and careful scholarship. So how does the reality of the text hold up to the pretense? I'm sure you can already guess, but let me give some examples to make clear what I learned by reading.

Rhetorically, this introduction to the critique does a lot of work, principally in setting up the way the reader should view Lomborg. He will go on to provide reasons (his examples) for dismissing Lomborg's conclusions. But his first reason given is an ethotic one, derived from the wondering about Lomborg's absence from previous debates on such issues (he has not earned credentials through experience) and his lack of contribution to the *scientific* literature on the subject. The implication is that Lomborg is not a scientist and has not earned his "stripes" in the field, as it were. Clearly, this is an attack against the person, aimed at weakening his credibility in the minds of the audience before any of Lomborg's actual arguments have been considered. This type of *ad hominem* argument appears as the counterside to the *ad verecundiam*, or Appeal to Authority, that we will see in Chapter 7: it strives to challenge expertise rather than draw from it.

But has something gone wrong here? Has the arguer committed a fallacy? We may be uncomfortable with the tone and some of the terms used to describe Lomborg and his work, and there is a sense that Lomborg is being dismissed as a serious consideration even *before* his arguments have been reviewed. But his arguments will be reviewed, so the strategy here plays only a contributory role in the author's overall case against Lomborg. And it does matter what credentials Lomborg has if he is presenting his research as scientifically important. So some circumstance of Lomborg – his lack of previous standing in and contributions to the field – is being used in an attack against him. Here, the *ad hominem* attack seems appropriate, or at least it can be defended. This is the kind of defense we will look for – the relevance of the circumstances being exposed to the arguments presented by the person attacked.

Case 5B

The next example is from a news report of a controversy surrounding Prince Charles ("Charles Faces Storm over Sex Scandal," reported in the *Globe and Mail*, November 8, 2003, p. A8), when allegations of sexual impropriety were brought against him by his former footman George Smith. Charles's private secretary, Sir Michael Peat, spoke out in his defense. You can extract Peat's argument from the following report:

Anyone who knows the Prince of Wales at all would appreciate that the allegation is totally ludicrous, and indeed, risible.

" ... the person who made the allegations 'has suffered health problems and has made other unrelated allegations which have been investigated by the police and found to be unsubstantiated.'"

He added that the former employee had suffered from alcoholism and posttraumatic stress disorder after serving in the forces in the Falkland Islands.

The ethotic reasoning here is complex. It includes an appeal to Charles's own good character. But the thrust of the defense involves an attack on the accuser's character. Charles's accuser has suffered health problems; has made unsubstantiated, though unrelated, accusations in the past; and has suffered from alcoholism and posttraumatic stress disorder (perhaps the last two points are a fuller explanation of the health problems first mentioned). Peat's argument would seem to be the following:

Premise: Features of Charles's accuser's character render him unreliable.
Conclusion: Charles's accuser's allegations should be dismissed (are totally ludicrous).

Granted, there is in addition here the premise addressing Charles's good character, but that itself would not be enough if the concerns about the accuser were not introduced. Unlike in the previous example, this is no preliminary focusing of the audience before the actual allegations are appraised. Implicit here is the suggestion that the allegations do not warrant appraisal because the accuser is unreliable. This better fits the basic form of the *argumentum ad hominem* as we see it in modern treatments. And it echoes the strategy that Aristotle had observed: the response is directed against the person, not the argument.

3 Treatments of *Ad Hominem*

We need to consider exactly what is problematic about fallacious *ad hominem* arguments. Certainly, they build on our natural tendency to connect what is said with the person or people saying it. In fact, part of our interest in dealing with the contexts of ordinary arguments requires us to do this. But for the most part we do this in order to appreciate fully what is said rather than as a way of dismissing what is said, unless it directly bears on what is said and provides grounds for that dismissal. Theorists are careful to distinguish between simple attacks on character – X is a known drunk so X is a bad person – and the questioning of a person's argument or advocacy of a proposition because of some characteristic or circumstance of the person. Brinton[4] draws attention to three elements that might be confused: the person, the person's advocacy of a proposition or claim, and the proposition or claim itself. A nonfallacious case of *ad hominem* argument would then be one that tried to influence an audience's attitudes to the person's advocacy of the proposition or claim by introducing relevant information about the person.

From this perspective, *fallacious* cases of *ad hominem* arguments would be ones that denied a claim or proposition in question solely on the basis of a person's advocacy of it – which is to say that all a good *ad hominem* argument could do is show that a person's advocacy of a claim is not a good reason for believing the claim; it does not show that the claim is false. So, the form

Premise: Person X advocates Y.

Premise: Person X is unreliable, untrustworthy, or otherwise
             flawed.

---

[4] Alan Brinton, "The *Ad Hominem*," in *Fallacies: Classical and Contemporary Readings*, edited by Hans V. Hansen and Robert C. Pinto (University Park, PA: Penn State University Press, 1995), p. 214.

Conclusion: Y is false

would be fallacious. The appropriate conclusion in such a case is something like the following:

Conclusion: Y cannot be believed on the basis of X's advocacy of it.

To illustrate what is at stake here, consider the following:

Case 5C

X has claimed Y. But how can that be true? After all, X has a history of making outrageous claims, not one of which has turned out to be justified.

Indeed, X's history may indeed lead us not to trust him this time. But that does not directly bear on the truth of Y, only on our reasons for believing it on the basis of X's say-so.

Another source for fallacious *ad hominem* arguments would focus on the relationship of what is being attributed to the person or claimed about her character and the position or argument she is advocating. If what is alleged about a person has no bearing on that person's advocacy of a claim, then the argument is flawed. Here we could have the form of argument we were looking for earlier, with the correct conclusion, but the argument would be deemed fallacious because what was introduced in the second premise was irrelevant to the person's argument. X may be a lawyer, for example, whose advocacy of a claim involves a particular interpretation of some aspect of family law. That X has a history of family problems is not relevant to his legal expertise in the case.

Finally here, we might consider how the *argumentum ad hominem* is seen to arise as a problem in dialogues that aim to resolve a dispute. For this we can review the position of the pragma-dialecticians, who introduce rules for the correct resolution of disputes and see fallacies as violations of those rules.[5] At

---

[5] In Chapter 1 we saw this as one way in which 'fallacy' can be defined.

several stages of a dispute, one or both parties may act so as to impede the expression or criticism of a standpoint. From this perspective, the various types of *ad hominem* that we are considering later are all attempts to prevent someone from speaking or advancing his view, either by denigrating him in some way, questioning his impartiality, or claiming an inconsistency.[6] Noteworthy here is that while other modern treatments now allow that the *ad hominem* can be a legitimate strategy in argument if the right conditions are met, the pragma-dialecticians' position is far more traditional in that it considers its use *always* to be fallacious. Hence, there is no need to sift through each case, deciding it on its merits. It is explicit in this account, though, that the person advancing an *ad hominem* does not deal with the other's argumentation but attempts to discredit that person by questioning his credibility.[7] So defined, any instance of the *ad hominem* would be fallacious, but not completely in the two ways we have just reviewed. Since in a case such as 5A a person may *both* attempt to discredit someone *and* deal with her or his argument, and since we have seen ways in which the attempt to discredit may itself be appropriate, we will add the pragma-dialecticians' concerns to our list of problems rather than agreeing that all *ad hominem* arguments are fallacious. We still need to take the time to decide whether an attack on a person in an argumentative debate has merits.

To review the discussion so far, we have identified three general problems with fallacious *ad hominem* arguments:

1. An arguer concludes that a person's position is false on the basis of introducing material that questions the person's

---

[6] Frans van Eemeren and Rob Grootendorst, "*Argumentum Ad Hominem*: A Pragma-Dialectical Case in Point," in *Fallacies: Classical and Contemporary Readings*, edited by Hans V. Hansen and Robert C. Pinto (University Park, PA: Penn State University Press, 1995), p. 225.

[7] Fran van Eemeren and Rob Grootendorst, *A Systematic Theory of Argumentation* (Cambridge: Cambridge University Press, 2004), p. 177.

credibility. This is a case of concluding too much, since the most that can be shown is that the person's advocacy of the position is not enough to warrant believing it.

2. The features of the person's character to which the arguer draws attention are irrelevant to the position that person is advocating. This is a case of introducing irrelevant considerations.

3. In the context of a dialogue, an arguer attempts to prevent another party from advancing her view by attacking her in some way and not addressing her view. This is a case of ignoring the issue in favour of addressing the person instead.

These concerns run the gambit from complete irrelevance, to concern about the premises, to concern about the conclusion. As will be clear from the few that have been surveyed, not all theorists will agree that all these concerns are appropriate or that they are of equal importance. But for a comprehensive review of the fallacy, we should bear all these things in mind and ask Critical Questions drawn from them as we appraise examples.

Critical Questions

1. Has an attack been made on another person in an argumentative debate?

2. Has that attack focused on the person's character or circumstance and avoided any discussion of his argument?

3. Where a conclusion has been drawn about the opponent's position or claim, is the *ad hominem* material introduced in the premises relevant to your appraisal of the position or claim, and are there grounds for believing the material is factually correct?

4. Where the *ad hominem* material is relevant, is the conclusion drawn from it appropriate?

As with Critical Questions in earlier chapters, these are intended to help you find your way through examples and build your evaluations. The first question is one of identity. Do we have an argument that fits the basic pattern of concern, where attention is drawn to the person delivering an argument or claim? Other candidates for confusion here will be ethotic arguments that involve appeals to the characters of others, or to their authority or expertise. But there the appeal is positive; here it is negative. Crucial to considering question 1, then, is the idea of an 'attack'. Much argumentation does arise in antagonistic conflicts. This has largely led to a regrettable situation in which argument itself is seen to be modeled on war and characterized by war metaphors. Certainly, talk of 'attacks' and 'opponents' supports this view. But as arguments are used constructively in social debates, this has become a dated model and much attention has been drawn to cooperative models of argument. Still, within such positive approaches not only can fallacies arise, but we will also see cases in which attention is drawn to a person's character or circumstances. So what is of interest to us here is really the *shift* from position to person. Drawing attention, negatively, to features of character may not involve an 'attack' in the traditional sense, and this will be enough for us to offer an affirmative answer to the first question.

The second question begins to focus our attention on what may be wrong with such an argument. Completely avoiding the person's argument or claim and addressing the person is a serious problem of irrelevance. No matter what flaws a person may have, she still deserves to have her argument considered and other people in the debate have an obligation to allow that argument to be expressed.[8] As van Eemeren and Grootendorst (2004, p. 178) point out, such attempts to silence the other party are usually directed for the benefit of an on-looking audience and with the intent to strengthen

---

[8] Consider how difficult the consequences of such a principle might be. It commits us to listening to people whose positions we may thoroughly oppose and deem to be without any merit, such as Holocaust deniers.

the silencer's own position. When audiences are alert to this, its inappropriateness becomes clear.

We still want to allow for cases in which the other's position is not simply ignored but is also considered and dismissed because of some feature of its proponent's character. Question 3 focuses on this pivotal concern and asks about the relevance of the _ad hominem_ material to the position being advanced. This will be the most difficult question to consider, as you weigh the nature of the position and of what is alleged about the character or circumstances of the person proposing it. Generally, the character claim must have a direct bearing on the person's position such that it would lead a reasonable person to question the position because of the connection. As with other relevance considerations, distributed throughout the evaluations of this book, proficiency will only develop as you practice working with the ideas and discussing cases with others.

You will note that in the earlier discussions of the chapter nothing was said about the 'truth' of what is being alleged in an _ad hominem_ argument. This is not an unimportant consideration; it is just difficult to determine in many cases. But it is possible that the _ad hominem_ material introduced is relevant to the position the person holds and yet we have grounds to believe that the material is factually incorrect. This is another matter of 'burden of proof'. In any _ad hominem_ argument, the person making the allegations has the obligation to support them with real evidence. Where this obligation has not been met, the argument is minimally a weak one (pending the arguer's ability to provide what is needed) and is likely fallacious.

Finally, it is important that _ad hominem_ arguments are seen for the kinds of contributory arguments to a case that they are. That is, they will not in themselves show a position to be wrong; they just weaken our reasons for holding that position because of the character flaws of the person advancing it. So the person advancing the _ad hominem_ argument can conclude no more than that a conclusion should not be accepted on the grounds that some discredited person asserts it. To argue more than this is to argue fallaciously.

4 Types of *Ad Hominem*

Having reviewed the general nature of *ad hominem* reasoning and the Critical Questions that will help us to appraise it, we now turn briefly to some of the subspecies of the *ad hominem*. We will review the abusive *ad hominem*, the circumstantial *ad hominem*, along with the *tu quoque*, and Guilt by Association.

Abusive *Ad Hominem*

As its name suggests, the abusive *ad hominem* involves a direct attack on an individual's character rather than some circumstance related to him. It is this variety of the fallacy that has probably caused the *ad hominem* to be generally dismissed as an appropriate strategy in argument, because such highly charged attacks, often accompanied by abusive language, are unlikely to impress anyone looking for good reasons. Such arguments are also more likely to fail the second of our critical questions and avoid altogether the person's argument. But we must also be careful that an actual argument is present. Calling someone names, while counterproductive to good communication, is not itself fallacious. So we need to be sure that the person has provided both premises and a conclusion. This is where many apparent abusive *ad hominem* arguments will fall by the wayside, because it will be difficult to construct fairly an argument from what has been said. The following example illustrates what is at stake in an argumentative context:

Case 5D

In February 2004, the Canadian biathlete and winner of two Olympic gold medals Myriam Bédard was embroiled in controversy when she claimed that the national passenger train company (Via Rail), for which she worked, had been overbilled by a marketing company. In a Montreal daily *La Presse* report (February 2004), Mr. Jean Pelletier, former chairman of Via Rail, accused Bédard of lying.

[Mr. Pelletier insisted Ms. Bédard's claim that Groupaction Marketing Inc. often over-billed Via Rail should not be believed.] "I don't want to be mean, but this is a poor girl who deserves pity, who doesn't have a spouse, as far as I know," he said. "She is struggling as a single mother with economic responsibilities. Deep down, I think she is pitiful."

Rather than address Ms. Bédard's charges, Pelletier chooses to attack her personally because she is a single mother who deserves pity. But he is offering an argument: he is somehow proposing that these facts about her are grounds not to believe what she says. His abusive *ad hominem* fails the third of our earlier critical questions: he draws a conclusion about her position (it should be disbelieved), but the reasons provided are quite irrelevant to it and so his *ad hominem* argument is fallacious.

   Looking back at Case 5B, you can now see that Peat's *ad hominem* against Prince Charles's accuser follows a similar path in dismissing the accusation because the person is a known drunk and has made inaccurate claims in the past. Each case must be decided on its own merits, and this one might have merit if the past claims are a matter of record. The burden of proof, however, lies with the arguer to provide this support. Otherwise, what we have is another fallacious argument.

Circumstantial *Ad Hominem*

The kind of *ad hominem* argument identified by John Locke is quite unlike the abusive variety. As you will recall, Locke saw the argument as one in which a person is pressed with "consequences drawn from his principles or concessions." This is to look not so much at a person's character as his particular circumstances relative to the issue in question. He may be in a position to benefit in some way from the way the case is resolved. Thus, bringing such a vested interest to light is to question an individual's position or argument for circumstantial reasons. The city planner who advocates building a new road along route A rather than route B may have her judgment questioned if an opponent points out that the planner happens to live along route B. The planner may present a very good case for why the road should follow route A, so an evaluator would have to consider carefully the degree to which the circumstantial factor should play a role in the reasoning. But this can be done by following the earlier Critical Questions. A particular kind of circumstance is often singled out under the separate heading of the *tu quoque*.

Tu Quoque Arguments

Tu quoque translates as "you too," and effectively suggests that there is an inconsistency between what a person does and what he says, or what he has said in the past and what he is proposing now. That is, the person is guilty of the very charge he is now making. The inconsistency here is pragmatic rather than logical. Typical examples would be dismissing the argument of a physician that you should diet because the physician is clearly overweight. Strictly speaking, the physician's own circumstances have no bearing on your own health. Another example could involve dismissing someone's criticism of your action because the critic has done exactly the same thing in the past. As Trudy Govier[9] has pointed out, while what someone has done may not have a bearing

[9] Trudy Govier, "Philosophy, Life and Philosophies of Life," *Philosophy Now* 49 (2005), pp. 23–25.

on the truth of what she claims, it may well be relevant to her personal credibility. In ethotic reasoning, where the credibility of the arguer is a key factor in considering what weight to give to his conclusion (perhaps because we have no better way to assess the truth of the claim), then the consistency of actions and words may be quite important. Consider how important it is for Socrates in Plato's *Apology* to demonstrate that his actions were consistent with what he believed, when dealing with different governments and when proposing a reward rather than a punishment after he had been found guilty at his trial. All this is to indicate that as appraisers we will need to consider carefully how important the consistency of character is in a particular argument.

Of course, people do and should change their minds (that is why we present arguments to them), so we cannot assume that because what a person advocates now is inconsistent with what she said in the past, she is violating some principle of consistency. We need to consider whether it is likely that she has changed her position. We also need to be sure that the alleged inconsistency is credible – that there is not some difference between the earlier case and the present.

Consider the following example drawn from a newspaper report of a debate in a state legislature:

Case 5E

Majority member Joe C. is under fire for using public funds to pay for more than $44,000 in expenses. Minority members accused the majority floor leader of having one standard in opposition and quite another standard in government. In defense of Joe C., the majority floor leader pointed out that a minority member (while in the previous majority) had himself been questioned about his expenses, including out of state travel expenses.

Note that both parties to this dispute are employing a *tu quoque*, one in attack and the other in defense. The critics of the majority floor leader accuse him of inconsistency in that he seems to be prepared to defend the very behaviour that he attacked when he was in the minority ranks. In defense the majority leader claims "You too" and points to the behaviour of one of the critics' own people when they formed the majority; the implication is that they too were prepared earlier to defend behaviour that they now are attacking. Such back-and-forth accusations serve only to impede any resolution of the issue and involve the kind of ignoring the issue that was captured in our earlier Critical Questions.

Guilt by Association

A final attack upon a person that we will consider is one based on some real or alleged association that person has, whether that association be with another person, organization, or way of thinking. The attack assumes that any "guilt" that characterizes the other part of the association can be transferred to the person making the argument. We saw two examples of just this kind of reasoning in Case 1A in Chapter 1. In that case Bjørn Lomborg's book *The Skeptical Environmentalist* was dismissed on the grounds of an imputed association with two books published in the 1970s that dealt with aliens who had allegedly built the pyramids and the mysteries of the Bermuda Triangle. Then the book's publisher, Cambridge University Press, was alleged to have tarnished its reputation by its association with the book. As we saw in our brief assessment of the arguments, the fallacy 'Guilt by Association' was committed in both instances. In the first charge, even if we allow some kind of 'guilt' (presumably unscientific speculation) to attach to the two books cited, no association between the books and Lomborg's work was shown. Hence, there was no transfer of guilt. As for the second charge, while clearly the association between Lomborg's book and its publisher does exist, since no guilt supported the first claim, there was none to transfer in the second. We can now see that the two charges made in that case, against Lomborg (via his book) and against the press, were types of *ad hominem* arguments in that they were against the reputations of each, although the sense of dismissing a position was not present in the charge against the press.

For the most part, Guilt by Association arguments can be evaluated for fallaciousness by using the basic Critical Questions presented earlier. With respect to the first question, we would be interested in seeing that the alleged association with a guilty party really did exist. With respect to the second question, we would look to see whether attention was being diverted away from the position. And with respect to the third question, we would test the relevance of the association to the position the person was advancing. The last question would be applied just as it was to earlier cases.

The general and specific kinds of *ad hominem* argument that have been discussed in this chapter all serve to illustrate further the need to explore carefully the contexts of argumentation when appraising fallaciousness. They also illustrate the two basic problems that we have recognized with fallacious arguments. The one problem has to do with the internal relationships of the argument's components. Asking whether the appropriate conclusion has been drawn from the *ad hominem* material captures this concern. The second basic problem has to do with the external relationships between the argument and its context and audience. Considerations of a person's character or circumstances and silencing of a party in the face of an audience speak to this general sense of fallaciousness.

CHAPTER EXERCISES

Set out the arguments in the following passages and evaluate them according to the discussions and Critical Questions of this chapter.

Not all cases will provide a clear *ad hominem* argument, and those that do may not be fallacious.

1. A recent letter from a local furrier presents a very eloquent attack on Humans United for Animal Protection. But the writer's arguments should not bear considering since they are from a man who clearly stands to gain from the continued trapping of defenseless animals.

2. Nicholas Lezard, *Guardian Weekly*, October 12, 1997:

   Edward de Bono's *Textbook of Wisdom*: This book contains some of the most mindless rubbish I've ever been privileged to hear from an adult. (If they'd called it "De Bono's Textbook of Risible Platitudes," that would have been fine.) I won't quote any because cleaning vomit from computer keyboards is nasty, time-consuming work. Just trust me when I say that you will become wiser if you gently smear your nose against any section of this newspaper – adverts included. No correspondence, please.

3. From Richard A. Posner, "Torture, Terrorism, and Interrogation" in Sanford Levinson, ed., *Torture: A Collection* (Oxford: Oxford University Press, 2004), p. 295:

   The issue is sharply posed by the chapter on torture in Alan Dershowitz's recent book on terrorism. I agree with much of what he says in that chapter. He says what only the most doctrinaire civil libertarians (not that there aren't plenty of them) deny, that if the stakes are high enough torture is permissible. No one who doubts that should be in a position of responsibility.

4. From a letter to the *Globe and Mail*, February 27, 1997:

   Peter Meisenheimer argues that the video recently released by the International Fund for Animal Welfare portrays "brutality" at the seal hunt, thus, presumably, justifying IFAW's continuing international media campaigns against the people of the Arctic and Atlantic Canada (letters – Feb. 15)....Mr. Meisenheimer's arguments would be more credible if he had indicated that the International Marine Mammal Association, which he claims to represent as a "research ecologist," in fact received funding of close to $300,000 from the IFAW in 1995.

5. The following is a letter to *National Geographic*, May 1998, responding to an article on the aviator Amelia Earhart, who disappeared in July 1937 while on a flight over the Pacific:

I have been researching women pilots for over ten years, and I was sorry to see Elinor Smith quoted, impugning Amelia's flying skills, in the otherwise excellent piece by Virginia Morell. Smith has been slinging mud at Earhart and her husband, George Putnam, for years, and I lay it down to jealousy. Amelia got her pilot's license in 1923 (not 1929 as Smith once wrote) and in 1929 was the third American woman to win a commercial license.

6. The following is a letter from a doctor of veterinary medicine (*Globe and Mail*, November 23, 2004, p. A14):

A Freelance writer dismisses her veterinarian's rational approach and takes her cat to a chiropractor, a man who began his vocation by "treating animals on the side." He's a fortunate fellow to arrive at his current level of experience without the long years of scientific education needlessly inflicted on veterinarians.

It comes as no surprise to learn that the cause of the cat's predicament is that "her spine is out of alignment." It is the only diagnosis ever proffered by chiropractors, regardless of the ailment.

The notion upon which chiropractic is based, the "subluxated vertebra," has yet to be shown to exist other than in the imagination of chiropractors. Dr. Leo Rosenberg and his profession are personifications of the adage that, to the person with only a hammer, every problem is interpreted as a nail. And at $100 for the first visit, a very expensive nail at that.

7. From a letter to jpost.com, July 11, 2004, accessed July 13, 2004, http://www.jpost.com/Letters/52630.html:

Did someone realize that:
1, The president of the International Court in Hague is a judge from China, a country on the forefront of "Human Rights" and "Justice" in the world?

A country well known for its "respect" for the rights of its minorities, and their religious, social, cultural and legal freedoms.

It would be quite interesting for a reporter to do some research about the justice imparted by the same judge, while on the bench in China, especially when dealing with political and religious dissidents.

8. From Charles Sanders Peirce (1960), *Collected Papers of Charles Sanders Peirce: Scientific Metaphysics*, Vol. 6, Charles Hartshorne and Paul Weiss (Eds.) (Cambridge, MA: Belknap Press of Harvard University Press, 1960), Chapter 4, "Answers to Questions Concerning My Belief in God," pp. 350–351:

Hume's argument [against miracles] is in no particularly intimate relation to the rest of his book, and was evidently inserted as a bid for popularity. For while he was a young fellow of fifteen to seventeen, miracles had been vehemently attacked by a clergyman of the name of Woolston, who took the ground of Origen and other early fathers of the church that the stories in the gospel were simply allegorical. His books had the most stupendous sale in England, completely demonstrating the general disbelief in miracles at that day. In point of fact, there never was a period in history in which the general tone of thought was so absolutely contrary to the supernatural. The state of opinion about [the time of] French Revolution, and that about 1875, when "agnosticism" was at its [crudest], were pious in comparison with 1730. Therefore, Hume who sacrificed the best parts of his system to make his *Inquiry* popular, undoubtedly stuck in his argument against miracles for that purpose.

9. The following is from a transcript of the presidential debate between President George W. Bush (R) and Sen. John F. Kerry (D). The moderator of the nationally televised debate was Jim Lehrer of PBS, September 30, 2004, text from FDCH E-Media, *The Washington Post*, accessed August 20, 2005, www.washingtonpost. com/wp-srv/politics/debatereferee/debate_0930html:

Bush: My opponent just said something amazing. He said Osama bin Laden uses the invasion of Iraq as an excuse to spread hatred for

America. Osama bin Laden isn't going to determine how we defend ourselves.

Osama bin Laden doesn't get to decide. The American people decide.

I decided the right action was in Iraq. My opponent calls it a mistake. It wasn't a mistake. He said I misled on Iraq. I don't think he was misleading when he called Iraq a grave threat in the fall of 2002.

I don't think he was misleading when he said that it was right to disarm Iraq in the spring of 2003.

I don't think he misled you when he said that, you know, anyone who doubted whether the world was better off without Saddam Hussein in power didn't have the judgment to be president. I don't think he was misleading.

I think what is misleading is to say you can lead and succeed in Iraq if you keep changing your positions on this war. And he has. As the politics change, his positions change. And that's not how a commander in chief acts.

Let me finish.

The intelligence I looked at was the same intelligence my opponent looked at, the very same intelligence. And when I stood up there and spoke to the Congress, I was speaking off the same intelligence he looked at to make his decisions to support the authorization of force.

Lehrer: Thirty seconds. We'll do a 30 second here.

Kerry: I wasn't misleading when I said he was a threat. Nor was I misleading on the day that the president decided to go to war when I said that he had made a mistake in not building strong alliances and that I would have preferred that he did more diplomacy. I've had one position, one consistent position, that Saddam Hussein was a threat. There was a right way to disarm him and a wrong way. And the president chose the wrong way.

Lehrer: Thirty seconds, Mr. President.

Bush: The only consistent [sic] about my opponent's position is that he's been inconsistent. He changes positions. And you cannot change positions in this war on terror if you expect to win.

10. From the same debate:

    Bush: Again, I can't tell you how big a mistake I think that is, to have bilateral talks with North Korea. It's precisely what Kim Jong Il wants. It will cause the six-party talks to evaporate. It will mean that China no longer is involved in convincing, along with us, for Kim Jong Il to get rid of his weapons. It's a big mistake to do that. We must have China's leverage on Kim Jong Il, besides ourselves. And if you enter bilateral talks, they'll be happy to walk away from the table. I don't think that'll work. . . .

    Kerry: Now, I'd like to come back for a quick moment, if I can, to that issue about China and the talks. Because that's one of the most critical issues here: North Korea.

    Just because the president says it can't be done, that you'd lose China, doesn't mean it can't be done. I mean, this is the president who said "There were weapons of mass destruction," said "Mission accomplished," said we could fight the war on the cheap – none of which were true.

    We could have bilateral talks with Kim Jong Il. And we can get those weapons at the same time as we get China. Because China has an interest in the outcome, too.

11. The following is the text of a full-page advertisement placed by ConsumerFreedom.com in *The New York Times Magazine*, February 27, 2005, accessed February 28, 2005:

    "Even if animal research resulted in a cure for AIDS, we'd be against it." – Ingrid Newkirk, President and co-founder People for the Ethical Treatment of Animals, quoted in *U.S.A. Today*. PETA's violent opposition to medical research is well known. Not well recognized: PETA has funded over $100,000 to criminals convicted of destroying medical research and firebombing scientific laboratories in the name of "animal liberation."

FURTHER READING

Ad Hominem arguments have received a lot of attention recently and the literature is well worth exploring in more detail. An excellent place to start is Douglas Walton's *Ad Hominem Arguments* (Tuscaloosa: University of Alabama Press, 1998). For competing views on the *ad hominem* see Brinton's ("The *Ad Hominem*") and van Eemeren and Grootendorst's ("*Argumentum Ad Hominem*: A Pragma-Dialectical Case in Point") chapters in *Fallacies: Classical and Contemporary Readings*, edited by Hans V. Hansen and Robert C. Pinto (University Park, PA: Penn State University Press, 1995). Trudy Govier's "Philosophy, Life and Philosophies of Life," *Philosophy Now* 49 (2005), pp. 23–25, gives an interesting historical case of *ad hominem* dispute among several philosophers.

CHAPTER 6

Other *'Ad'* Arguments

1 Introduction

Over time, the arguments *'ad'*, as we might call them, have become quite a sizable group. As a genre they arose with Locke, but logicians have felt free to add to them, particularly throughout the last two centuries. Hence, Hamblin[1] provides a list that includes the *argumenta ad fidem* (Faith), *superbiam* (Pride), *odium* (Hatred), *amicitiam* (Friendship), *invidiam* (Envy), and many more. In this chapter, we will explore four of the more frequently occurring *'ad'* fallacies, the *argumenta ad populum* (Popularity), *baculum* (Force), *misericordiam* (Pity), and *Ignorantiam* (Ignorance). Then, in the next chapter, we will consider the *argumentum ad verecundiam*, now treated as the Appeal to Authority, in more detail.

What the *'ad'* fallacies have in common, besides names derived from Latin terms, is that they are appeals to some contextual factors that characterize the type of argument involved. These factors give some clues to where we might expect to meet them. The *ad baculum*, for example, often arises in confrontations or arguments

---

[1] Charles L. Hamblin, *Fallacies* (London: Methuen, 1970), p. 41.

in which some kind of power or authority is asserted. The *ad misericordiam* occurs in contexts in which some special consideration is being sought on emotional grounds. And the *ad ignorantiam* is frequently found in inquiries in which knowledge claims are being advanced. As does the *ad hominem* of the previous chapter, these fallacies arise in the processes of argumentation itself.

2 | *Argumentum Ad Populum*

There is an old adage to the effect that "thousands of people can't be wrong." And yet, as we frequently learn to our chagrin, thousands of people often are wrong: they support dictators, engage in unhealthy lifestyles, or put their money into schemes that seem to have little chance of success. All this leads us to ask what weight we should place on such popularity when it is advanced in support of a cause or claim. Where the weight is unwarranted the argument commits the *ad populum* fallacy, or an illicit appeal to popularity. In its most overt cases it will claim 'X is true because many (most; thousands; all) people believe X'. Of course, people may well have good reasons for what they believe (belief in gravity, for example), but generally it is difficult to infer the truth of a claim from the number of people who believe it. We do, however, need to consider carefully what grounds the popularity and how it is related to what is being claimed.

We must also appreciate that much argumentation depends on establishing a connection with an audience by appealing to things they will find acceptable or hold to be common knowledge, and one reason for accepting something is that it is generally held by others. Hence, we cannot identify all Appeals to Popularity as *ad populum* fallacies in the way some in the textbook tradition have. If the claim about what people believe is the result of a scientifically conducted opinion poll, for example, then it is reasonable to give some weight to it. Consider the following case:

Case 6A

The following is a letter to the editor dealing with the funding of stem cell research. It is found at http://www.lifesite.net/interim/2002/july/letters.html:

For the non-elected staff at the Ottawa Research Institute to get grants of millions of dollars, to do their own thing "in the still-controversial field of stem cell research" shows that the OHRI thinks that "might is right." Most taxpayers oppose experimenting on embryo stem cells because the scientific fact is that we are dealing with human life. Slow down OHRI and be aware of the fact that most taxpayers are in favour of research on adult stem cells but are totally opposed to research on embryo stem cells. Are ya listening?

Several related conclusions might be attributed to the arguer here: the person opposes the research on embryo stem cells being conducted by the Ottawa Research Institute using taxpayers' money, and the arguer advocates the use of adult stem cells in their stead. However we understand the claims, each is supported by a key premise that appeals to popular (taxpayer) opinion. Most taxpayers oppose embryonic stem cell research, and most taxpayers favor adult stem cell research. In fact, the opposition to embryonic stem cell research is reiterated with the stronger 'totally' attached to it.

This is a difficult case to consider because public opinion should have some input into public policies, if it is well informed. We would not, for example, favor acting on opinions if they were based on no more than prejudice. One of the problems in this case is that we have no way of knowing how well based the opinion is. In fact, people aware of the polling done around this issue will recognize that the evidence contradicts these premises altogether: "most" people do not oppose embryonic stem cells, and some who do are not 'totally' opposed but would base their opposition on the way the stem cells are obtained. The larger question here is whether the view of many is a relevant consideration when deciding what research to fund. That the views in question are those of taxpayers suggests that the arguer believes we should have some say in how our money is spent. But, generally, this is not a principle that is recognized; governments spend money on all kinds of programs without heed to taxpayer opinion. That people believe certain research is "wrong" and should not be funded is not itself a relevant reason for believing it to be wrong. Its rightness or wrongness must depend on something more. Such a something more may be suggested in the reference to human life, but any principle alluded to here needs to be made explicit.

This case shows how complex appeals to popular opinion can be. On the whole, it is not hard to see why they would deceive audiences in cases in which they are deceptive. There is a natural attraction to peer pressure in all walks of life, particularly with the advertising of consumer products. But that brand X detergent is the most popular in terms of monthly sales does not mean it is the best detergent. It only means, to risk the tautology here, that it is more popular than other brands. Its popularity could be due to its being cheaper, or more readily available, or it could be simply the result of successful marketing campaigns that associated it with an attractive lifestyle. So, we must weigh each appeal to popularity to determine how that appeal is grounded and what might reasonably be concluded from it.

The following Critical Questions are intended to assist us in this:

Critical Questions

1. Is the appeal to a popular belief or practice so widely known to be correct that the burden of proof would lie with anyone who questioned it?
2. If not, and the burden lies with the arguer, has the popularity been adequately supported or explained (by a poll, for example)?

3. Is the popularity relevant to the claim made in the conclusion?

The first question helps us assess whether we have an appeal to
popular opinion or to common knowledge. The latter is a concept
that refers to ideas, knowledge, and beliefs that an audience ought
to know given the environment of ideas, knowledge, and beliefs in
which they live. We cannot be sure that any particular member of
an audience *will* know such things, but it is reasonable to expect
him to if these things are commonly known. In the case of such
common knowledge, we can answer this question in favour of the
arguer.

If, however, it is a genuine appeal to popularity, then it matters
whether the arguer has supported it with the right kind of evidence.
The second question addresses this. What we are most particularly
looking for here is some kind of result from a poll that has been
scientifically conducted. The arguer in Case 6A seems to be assuming such a poll exists to support the premises there, but nothing
is provided. These polls themselves may involve some fallacious
reasoning, but we will tackle those questions in Chapter 8.

Now that we have established that we have the correct argument type and that the popularity premise is supported, the third
question then allows us to address the core issue of whether the
appeal to popularity is relevant to the conclusion in the context
of this argument. This involves considering why the popularity
exists at all and whether it is grounded in a way that increases the
likelihood of the conclusion's being true. If not, then the argument
commits the *ad populum* fallacy.

3 *Argumentum Ad Baculum*

When we turn to study the Appeal to Force or *ad baculum* we
find that many textbooks will make short work of this. How, after

all, can it be legitimate to reach a reasonable conclusion by means of a premise that evokes fear in an audience? But, again, we are on ground where we need to tread cautiously. Careful accounts of the argument scheme[2] and the fallacy[3] uncover a complexity that warns against hasty conclusions about such arguments. The *ad baculum* is literally an argument to the stick and seems to suggest beating persuasion into an audience. Clearly, an argument with the form 'If you don't accept/believe proposition P, I'll do X to you; therefore P is true' is nakedly fallacious. But then we must ask how anyone could be deceived by such arguments. Insofar as we want to consider fallacies that audiences could mistake for correct arguments, we need to look more closely at what is involved.

In fact, such appeals to force or fear fall under the umbrella of arguments from Negative Consequences (Walton, p. 283), in which people are moved by considerations of unpleasant or undesirable outcomes. If we are to take the *ad baculum* seriously, we need to look for it in contexts that allow and even expect threats or warnings. Arguments that deal with risk management, for example, will often warn of negative outcomes that may follow if certain options are pursued, and labour negotiations will involve threats of lock outs and strikes that are an expected part of the process engaged in by both parties. Similarly, we will find explicit or implicit threats in diplomatic arguments or those that arise between hostile parties during times of war. On *these* occasions, we might find an audience being deceived by fallacious reasoning if the appropriate conditions governing the rules of argumentation in those contexts are not followed or are broken.

---

[2] Douglas Walton, *Fundamentals of Critical Argumentation* (Cambridge: Cambridge University Press, 2006).

[3] John Woods, "Appeal to Force," in *Fallacies: Classical and Contemporary Readings*, edited by Hans V. Hansen and Robert C. Pinto (University Park, PA: Penn State University Press, 1995) pp.240–250.

In this respect, van Eemeren and Grootendorst's rules for resolving a critical discussion come to mind.[4] You will recall from Chapter 1 and some of the intervening discussions that on their model a fallacy is a violation of one of the rules. Insofar as the issuing of a threat appears as a way to prevent another party from advancing or criticizing a point, then whether it is done directly or indirectly, such a threat is a fallacious move in argument. Of course, we cannot conclude from this that threats will always involve attempts to avoid cooperation. As noted, threats that are integral to the procedures involved in negotiations, as long as they are supported by good reasons, may be intended to move the discussion cooperatively toward its conclusion.[5] Moreover, these same contexts provide another important element that will help us identify fallacious cases. It is central to such threats that the other party has a clear way to act so as to avoid the consequences of what is threatened. There must be some way in which the other can comply. With these ideas in mind, let us explore a case:

Case 6B

This case is from George W. Bush's speech to the nation just after the United States had initiated the attack on Afghanistan, October 7, 2001. The full transcript is available at http://archives.cnn.com/2001/US/10/07/ret.bush.transcript/.

More than two weeks ago, I gave Taliban leaders a series of clear and specific demands: Close terrorist training camps. Hand over leaders of the Al Qaeda network. And return all foreign nationals, including American citizens, unjustly detained in their country. None of these demands was met. And now, the Taliban will pay a price. By destroying camps and disrupting communications, we will make it more

---

[4] Fran van Eemeren and Rob Grootendorst, *A Systematic Theory of Argumentation* (Cambridge: Cambridge University Press, 2004).

[5] John Woods ("Appeal," p. 246) illustrates this point well in his discussion of the *ad baculum*.

difficult for the terror network to train new recruits and coordinate their evil plans. . . .

Today we focus on Afghanistan, but the battle is broader. Every nation has a choice to make. In this conflict, there is no neutral ground. If any government sponsors the outlaws and killers of innocents, they have become outlaws and murderers themselves. And they will take that lonely path at their own peril.

This excerpt gives us two instances of the *ad baculum*. In the first paragraph, Bush refers to an earlier set of demands that we might judge as threats and that were associated with specific consequences. The other party in the dispute, the Taliban regime in Afghanistan, has failed to comply and now the consequences are being put into place. This is not an argument that aims at establishing the truth of a claim or persuading the audience to hold a belief, at least not directly. Rather, Bush had made a commitment that he would act to see the promised negative consequences come about unless the other party carried out the course of action required. Critics may disagree with the political and military strategy involved and may rue the absence of an attempted diplomatic solution in favour of issuing a threat, but from the point of view of the argumentative strategy used it does not seem obviously fallacious. We have a context in which threats and counterthreats are the norm, the arguer is overt in what he is claiming, and there are clear ways for the other to comply.

Contrast this with the second paragraph. Here the threat is directed more obscurely at "every nation" whose government may sponsor outlaws and killers. The obscurity is compounded by the lack of any clear definition of "outlaw" and the questionable category claim that by sponsoring murderers, members of the government *become* murderers. The nature of the dispute here is less clear, the threat has no clear target, and compliance is impeded by the vagueness of the terms. This would then seem to be a candidate for a fallacious use of the argument.

The following Critical Questions will help us deal with the contextual complexities of such cases:

Critical Questions

1. Is this an argument in which a threat has been made insofar as negative consequences have been proposed or identified?
2. Is this a context in which such a strategy is appropriate according to the procedures usual in that context, and is the introduction of the threat relevant to the reasonable conduct of the process?
3. Are there clear ways for the other party to comply so as to avoid the negative consequences?

The first question seems straightforward but the answers may be complicated by some vagueness about what constitutes a threat and whether it is explicit or indirect. An arguer who simply points out consequences that might follow if a course of action were taken may claim if challenged that she is not threatening at all but simply highlighting matters by way of giving advice. Contextual matters will undoubtedly help us, so question 2 may enter into the answer to the first question.

Question 2 is the central one here. While not deciding in advance what contexts may admit of threats, some clear ones have already been identified and we can expect there to be others. Advertising, for example, in which we expect to be presented with the qualities of the product being advertised, would not seem an appropriate discourse for threats. Each case should be considered on its own merits and in light of what procedures would govern such a case. This will also allow us to see whether the threats have been introduced in a relevant way and at a relevant time. Do they contribute to the potential resolution of the dispute or question, or do they detract from it (by, say, threatening before the other party can explain his position)? If the latter, then the argument is fallacious.

The last question addresses the reasonableness of the demand or threat. In labour negotiations, can the one party reasonably avoid a lockout by agreeing to certain concessions, or is there no reasonable way in which she could comply because of the vagueness of the demand or its absolute nature? Again, this question may need to be taken in conjunction with the previous one. A mugger who threatens you with violence unless you hand over your valuables (a popular example in many textbooks) has given you a clear way to comply and avoid the negative consequences, but his 'argument' runs foul of the conditions in the second question.

4 *Argumentum Ad Misericordiam*

Emotional appeals are very common in reasoning. We often introduce our feelings into our argument because we have strong commitments or are deeply affected by what we take to be instances of injustice and the like. There is nothing wrong with this. Since the time of Aristotle logicians have recognized a role for emotions in arguments because arguers address audiences as whole people. But when attention is drawn away from what is actually at stake, or emotional appeals are substituted for good reasons, then we have candidates for fallacious arguments. Key among these is the *argumentum ad misericordiam*, or Appeal to Pity. The idea here is to draw attention to some circumstance affecting you or someone else and gain the pity of your audience, on the basis of which they are led to a conclusion that they would not otherwise have likely accepted.

Not all *ad misericordiam* arguments will be fallacious. There are circumstances in which it will be legitimate to awaken the appropriate sensibilities in an audience in order to induce them to think seriously about an issue and act accordingly. Arguably, television advertising that solicits monies for African children affected by acquired immunodeficiency syndrome (AIDS) by presenting images of such children and their atrocious conditions is following this strategy. Most of us would be loath to charge the organizations behind such advertising with fallacious arguing.

The conclusion drawn from an *ad misericordiam* is also important. The example just given would involve reasoning to take a certain action (giving money) rather than holding a belief about the way the world is. The television images may well cause us to form a correct belief about the impact of AIDS in Africa because they relay accurate information. But that is not due to the appeal to pity, which is designed to persuade us to act. The belief that AIDS affects children in Africa is a correct cognitive response to the image; our being emotionally moved to act on this is a response to the pity premise. It is difficult to imagine cases in which a pity premise is used to support a claim about what is the case,[6] and even more difficult to imagine audiences' being deceived by such an argument. More likely, the *ad misericordiam* arguments we encounter will conclude that some course of action is in order and we will need to judge the correctness of such arguments.

Consider the following kind of common case:

Case 6C

This is from a student request to a professor to reevaluate a course grade.

I have recently been informed by the Financial Aid Office that my final average of 78.6 is 0.9% below what I need (i.e. 79.5% or greater) to renew my $3500 Aiming for the Top Scholarship. I may not be able to return without this scholarship.

---

[6] See Douglas Walton, *Appeal to Pity: Argumentum ad Misericordian* (Albany: State University of New York Press, 1997), p. 152.

I am sending this e-mail to request you to review my final grade as it would greatly aid me in renewing my scholarship.

What is noteworthy here is that there is likely no attempt at deception by the student. As attached to the case as he is, he is as misled by the reasoning as any audience might be. This helps us to see how such reasoning can confuse us. The breakdown of the argument is quite simple. The action requested of the professor, or the conclusion, is a review of the final grade in the course. The reasons given for this conclusion are the factual premise indicating his grade average and the requirement for the scholarship, and the pity premise that without the scholarship the student may not be able to return to his studies.

What has gone wrong here should be clear. A relevant reason for reviewing the grade would be an academic one indicating that the grade had been miscalculated or was not representative of the student's performance or understanding in the course. Instead, the irrelevant reason of the student's unfortunate circumstance is all that is provided. Clearly, it would be unfair to other students in the course to start making arbitrary changes to grades that were not justified on academic grounds. Still, the emotional appeal could be such as to mislead someone into feeling sorry for the student and persuading him to act. Thus, it is not difficult to see how such appeals may work.

Critical questions for the *argumentum ad misericordiam* will need to distinguish legitimate from illegitimate strategies by focusing on the reasonableness of the claim being supported by the pity premise and the relevance of the pity premise to the claim. The following Critical Questions will accomplish this:

Critical Questions

1. Does the arguer appeal to pity in order to support the truth of a claim or recommend some action?

2. Is this a context in which emotional appeals are relevant?
3. Is the pity premise relevant to the conclusion being advanced?

The first question identifies the argument as an *ad misericordiam* and distinguishes the kinds of conclusion being supported. As noted earlier, the mere fact that a truth claim is asserted as a conclusion would not mean the argument is fallacious. But we might imagine few if any cases in which this holds, so this can be an indicator of fallaciousness.

The second question draws our attention to the context. In theory, emotional appeals may arise in any context as people advocate what they feel is important. But there are also contexts in which we would not expect arguers to appeal to pity and the occurrence of such appeals would make us think carefully about the appropriateness. If you are negotiating the terms of a loan and the bank's finance officer suddenly presses you to accept a higher interest rate because it will increase his standing with the bank and enable him to take his family to Disney World, you will find this an inappropriate interjection.

The last question is the crucial one in this set and will likely involve the most judgment. Is the pity premise relevant to what is being recommended in the conclusion? Since we are talking here about dialectical relevance to audiences and contexts, we must consider a full range of conditions and circumstances likely to be involved. A convicted felon's loss to his young family if he is incarcerated for a long time will be a consideration to the court at the time of sentencing, but not in establishment of guilt. The impoverished living conditions of the spouses of war veterans who are ineligible for specific benefits will be judged a relevant reason for extending those benefits to them, depending on how the unfairness of the situation has been established. But cases such as 6C will clearly fail to meet the third question and be judged fallacious because of it.

5 | *Argumentum Ad Ignorantiam*

The argument from ignorance or appeal to ignorance (*argumentum ad ignorantiam*) is said to have been first named by John Locke in the same short piece in which he discusses the *ad hominem*. But contemporary writers are at a loss to see the connections between modern treatments and what Locke has said. In this discussion, we will focus on the modern treatments.

Basically, the argumentative strategy in question involves drawing a conclusion on the basis of the absence of evidence against that conclusion – at least, that is the simplest form of the *ad ignorantiam*. For example, someone might use the absence of evidence disproving the existence of ghosts as proof *for* the claim that ghosts exist, on the grounds that if they did not, someone would have shown this by now. The following is an example of a pure *ad ignorantiam*:

Case 6D
If the tobacco industry truly believed it could commission a study to prove that advertising tobacco products does not affect consumption, it would have done so by now. Thus, advertising tobacco products does affect consumption.

Recalling a discussion from Chapter 3, you may note that this is a valid form of argument that we call 'Denying the Consequent'. The hidden premise is the denial of the consequent – the industry has not conducted such a study. But the fallaciousness lies in its being an argument that assumes a conclusion to be correct on the sole basis of the absence of evidence to suggest otherwise.

An interesting feature of this argumentative strategy is that it has the effect of reversing the burden of proof. We can imagine a dialectical exchange in which one party asks for proof of a claim and the other responds, "Well, you cannot prove that it isn't true." This shifting of the burden of proof is one of the reasons the *ad ignorantiam* has been judged fallacious.[7] The first speaker has avoided an obligation to provide proof by insisting that the other party cannot disprove the matter.

There is, though, a reasonable way of using this type of argument. In law courts, for example, the absence of evidence proving guilt is taken as evidence of innocence. And scientists establish tests for hypotheses in order to see whether hypotheses are true. The failure of the predicted consequences to arise from the test, that is, the failure to confirm, is taken as evidence against the hypothesis, which is a proof of disconfirmation.

These situations are significant in two respects. In the first instance, unlike in the simplest cases involving fallacy, in which the conclusion is quickly drawn, here the conclusion is drawn only after there has been a concerted effort through inquiry or testing to find the evidence. So the negative finding is appropriately supported. The other significant factor is that these legitimate types of *ad ignorantiam* involve not so much the absence of evidence for something as *negative* evidence against it. There is demonstrated evidence against X's truth; therefore, X must be false.

This is one of the problems of evidence that we have to weigh when reviewing *ad ignorantiam* arguments. The other is the standard of evidence that is being used. Consider the following case:

Case 6E

Many philosophers of religion and theologians argue that there exists religious knowledge as a domain of knowledge with its own claims and criteria for evaluation. Other philosophers, however, dispute the very existence of such knowledge on the grounds that it fails to meet the criteria of evidence appropriate to science. Here, the

---

[7] Erik C. W. Krabbe, "Appeal to Ignorance," in *Fallacies: Classical and Contemporary Readings*, edited by Hans V. Hansen and Robert C. Pinto (University Park, PA: Penn State University Press, 1995).

criteria of evidence in one domain (science) is used to criticize claims in another domain (religion). Does religious knowledge constitute a legitimate domain of knowledge, with its own propositions and criteria for evidence? The scientific response to such claims is that religious knowledge should count only if it can be presented in terms of scientific evidence and logic. That is, one field is required to submit to the standards of another field. But of course, the very point in the debate is that there are claimed to be two sets of standards.

It is not difficult to see how an *ad ignorantiam* argument could be drawn from this case. Proponents of the scientific model essentially argue that because religious knowledge cannot meet the standard of evidence of that model, then there is no 'evidence' for it, and on such terms its claims are false or meaningless. A better way for the scientist to proceed would be to evaluate the claims to religious knowledge on their own terms and according to their own criteria. But this may be to concede too much at the outset. There is, however, something problematic about the scientists' strategy. In terms of some of the rules for critical discussion that we have reviewed elsewhere, this seems tantamount to preventing one party from advancing her standpoint by excluding her in advance from the standards of discussion. At the same time, it seems that to allow the debate of the other party's terms is for the scientists to give up the very rules that they see governing the debate. This may be one of those intractable situations that we must sometimes live with while the debate addressing it moves along slowly toward some resolution.

What our discussion does bring to light are the important factors we must consider when investigating possible fallacious *ad ignorantiam* arguments. We are interested in conclusions that are drawn on the absence of evidence; confusing absence of evidence with negative evidence; and judging others with a failure to meet standards of evidence they were never equipped to meet.

Our Critical Questions for the *ad ignorantiam* will incorporate these ideas.

Critical Questions

1. Is a conclusion being drawn that something is or is not the case on the basis of an absence of evidence showing otherwise?
2. Has there been a reasonable effort to search for evidence, or is the absence of evidence for or against something really negative evidence arising from the attempts to show otherwise?
3. Are the expectations for what should count as evidence reasonable in the context?

The first Critical Question deals with identification. We are looking for the form of argument in which the premises refer to the absence of evidence for or against a claim. But the conclusion must then assert in some way that the issue is proved by the failure to show otherwise. The failure to show a "missing link" in the fossil record, for example, is taken as proof against such a link and the theory (evolution) that some believe requires it.

The identification issue goes further into the second question, because the absence of evidence for something may indeed be negative evidence that has been collected against it. In such cases, we do not have the jump in logic that the simple *ad ignorantiam* fallacy expresses (as in question 1). There may be a hasty conclusion, depending on how much negative evidence has been amassed, but then the fallacy is one of Hasty Generalization, which we will deal with in Chapter 8, and not *ad ignorantiam*. We will want to identify the argument as fallacious when there has been no real attempt to garner any evidence.

More difficult is deciding whether the expectation of what should count as evidence is reasonable in any particular case. We would look for instances in which the cards seem to be stacked in advance against the success of one party or a particular thesis. Your failure to lift a minimal amount of weight should reasonably count as evidence against the proposition that you are a serious bodybuilder. But it would be unfair to insist that you be fluently conversant with the entire Aristotelian corpus before you will be taken as a serious philosophy student, and then take the absence of such ability as evidence that you are not.

6 Summary

Arguments 'ad' are complex things, especially in their fallacious forms. The selection of such arguments we have investigated in this chapter involved very different features that require a wide array of contextual considerations when it comes to evaluation. They are also far from straightforward in the identification of what is wrong with them. But at the same time, we can see how the errors might arise in people's reasoning, and how audiences might be deceived by them. The next chapter will involve a fuller investigation of another of the key 'ad' arguments.

CHAPTER EXERCISES

Evaluate the following passages according to the ideas discussed in this chapter and the Critical Questions provided. Determine what type of 'ad' argument is involved and whether a fallacy has been committed, defending your judgment in each case. Not all cases may be fallacious instances of the arguments involved.

1. From an ad for Chrysler Minivans, *New York Review of Books*, June 11, 1992:

From day one, the first minivans have been the world's favorites. We invented the minivans in 1984, and they became the preferred family vehicles almost overnight. By now we've sold over three million, and we continue to outsell all the competition combined. If you own a Caravan, Voyager or Town & Country, you know why. The Front-wheel drive, the handling, the ride, the room, the comfort, the warranty — nobody has put the whole package together the way we have.

2. Background: In April 2005 several North American newspapers published unclear photographs that allegedly showed Bigfoot. The following is one skeptical response (*Globe and Mail*, Thursday, April 21, 2005, p. A14):

Re. Footage Shot in Manitoba Shows Bigfoot, Viewers Say (April 20): The Loch Ness monster, UFOs and other such "mysteries" have one thing in common – the shadowy, grainy photo.
   Considering how many hunters are combing North America every year, it seems highly unlikely that one of them wouldn't have shot a Bigfoot by now.

3. The following is from an advertising flyer promoting a security alarm system.

You don't have to be a statistic! The experts admit "It's not **IF** you will be the victim of a break-in... but **WHEN**." Astro-Guard security systems stops [*sic*] burglars *BEFORE* they get inside. Here are the frightening **FACTS** about crime in your community. ONE OUT OF FOUR! Those are the statistical chances of you and your family being the victims of a break-in **within the next 12 months**. Crime increased 52% last year over the year before. 95% of ASTRO-GUARD Security Systems are purchased by homeowners *after* a break-in has occurred. Most burglaries are committed by inexperienced juveniles and young adults who are intimidated by alarm sounds and lights. Insurance *cannot* replace heirlooms or sentimental treasures. Insurance *cannot* compensate the psychological trauma that often accompanies a break-in. Insurance *cannot* overcome the feeling of violation associated with a break-in or eliminate the injuries and suffering of an assault. Psychiatrists, Psychologists, Criminologists, Security Experts and Police Officials all agree: "THE EARLIER THE INTRUDER IS DISCOVERED, THE MORE EFFECTIVE THE SECURITY SYSTEM!"

4. The following is from a pamphlet issued by the Doris Day Animal League, 1992:

Issue #3 in your Animal Protection Poll is "pound seizure" – the practice of selling pound animals to research laboratories. Many of these animals were household pets, like your dog and cat. Some were abandoned. Others simply got lost. The Doris Day Animal League believes that pounds should care for these animals and work for their adoption into loving families – not sell them to laboratories where they will be tortured or killed.

5. In 1997, the British novelist Frederick Forsyth published a widely produced defense of foxhunting ("The Kindness of the Hunt," *New York Times*, July 19, 1997, reprinted, *Globe and Mail*, July 21, 1997, p. A15). The following is an example of responses to that article:

Frederick Forsyth claims that the campaign against fox hunting is merely one of political correctness. This is absurd. Millions of people abhor blood sports, and setting a pack of trained dogs against a single small animal, which is incapable of defending itself, is one of the worst examples of blood sports anywhere.

6. From a letter to the editor of the *Globe and Mail*, July 25, 1997, from the executive director of the Humane Society of Canada. This refers to the same article as the previous example:

Re. The Kindness of the Hunt (July 21): I read with deep concern the views expressed by well known fiction writer Frederick Forsyth, who defends fox hunting as a practice which helps farmers and is a useful conservation tool. Repeated public opinion polls have shown that seven out of 10 people in Britain believe that fox hunting is cruel and indiscriminate blood sport that should have been outlawed years ago.

. . . Each fall, an estimated 350 packs of hounds unleashed by their ridiculously dressed owners astride galloping steeds thunder across the English countryside. Their sole objective is to harass, chase and kill a terrified wild animal which weighs less than 20 pounds. As a part of their training the hounds are encouraged to develop their killer instincts by hunting fox cubs. Each year, fox hunting is responsible for the deaths of between 15,000 to 20,000 animals. This is a cowardly mob mentality at its very worst. However, because of a rational compassionate majority the trumpeting cry of this 250-year-old sport may soon be silenced forever.

7. From the *LA Times* online edition, accessed May 26 2004, http://www.latimes.com/news/opinion/letters/la-le-klatman23 may23,0,6895410.story?coll=la-news-comment-letters:

Re "Stem Cell Research on Course, Director Says," May 16: These are the lost years for people who need a cure for something. As the parents of the 2003–04 American Diabetes Assn.'s national youth advocate, Emma Klatman, 12, we pine for the day the cure for diabetes is found. But these lost years could spell horrendous diabetes complications for our daughter and millions of others whose lives have been cut short by the current administration's refusal to pursue promising research. According to 100 Nobel laureates and other serious intellectuals, and now Nancy Reagan, stem cell research must be pursued.

Eight times a day and sometimes more, and once or maybe twice each and every night, we poke our daughter's soft fingers to find out if she needs insulin or a cookie for "lows." Every time we test blood sugars, change an insulin pump site or administer yet another insulin dose, we remember that the National Institutes of Health's research billions and the millions of American taxpayers who might need a cure for something are bound up in the tangle of politics and religion. We pray that the cure is found without restraint.

8. From the *Independent* online, accessed July 1, 2004, http://argument.independent.co.uk/letters/story.jsp?story=535710:

Sir: Our society appears to accept that the individual has a duty to live, no matter how wretched his or her life is, no matter how little chance there is that things will ever improve and, above all, no matter whether that individual wants to go on living or not ("Couple who died in Swiss suicide clinic 'not terminally ill'," 23 June).

The Stokes were a devoted couple, with such poor physical health that they had to live in a care home. They both had a long history of psychiatric illness, and had made several thwarted attempts at suicide. Each dreaded outliving the other.

Shame on us and our laws that they had to travel to another country to find compassionate medical help to have a gentle death in each other's arms.

Sir: I am 96 years old and have suffered for many years from shortage of breath and other difficulties, and consequently I have "existed" not "lived," sitting in a chair most of the time.

I am now in a care home. The staff are most kind but this does not overcome the urge to do things, and as a result there have been one or two falls (fortunately incurring no damage except pain). I have prayed for years to be relieved from all this but present laws do not allow it. Given a controlled opportunity I, like many others, would have taken it. An "existence" like this benefits no one.

I realise that there must be strong overseeing and any loosening of the regulations has to be carefully looked into but, with an increasingly elderly population, surely it is time for the law to be changed.

9. From the *Observer/Guardian* online, accessed May 25 2004, http://observer.guardian.co.uk/letters/story/0,6903,1194278,00.html:

Andrew Anthony (Review, last week) starts by referring to God in heaven as a 'far-fetched idea'. But whatever it is, the belief of most of humanity can hardly be far-fetched. The small step he takes from disagreement to bigotry is the first step towards all the extremisms his trenchant article condemns. A joke maybe, but the worst bullies I knew were two atheists who would persecute a gentle Presbyterian colleague with jokes.

10. In Book X of his *Republic*, Plato banishes poetry from his state. Still, in spite of the ancient quarrel between poetry and philosophy, because of poetry's nature, Socrates (the speaker) allows that "if the poetry that aims at pleasure and imitation has any argument to bring forward that proves it ought to have a place in a well-governed city, we at least will be glad to admit it" (*Rep.* X 607c). The problem with this is that earlier (605a), it has been

determined that the imitative poet is related by nature to the inferior part of the soul and that poetry appeals to the inferior part and not to reason. Hence, if it were to do what Socrates now asks of it (present an argument) it would no longer be poetry.

FURTHER READING

The *'ad'* fallacies have become popular subjects of inquiry in the literature, especially with regard to the question of when these argument schemes are *not* fallacious. Students interested in reading more about them could not do better than begin with some of Douglas Walton's investigations: *Arguments from Ignorance* (University Park, PA: Penn State University Press, 1996); *Appeal to Pity: Argumentum ad Misericordiam* (Albany: State University of New York Press, 1997); *Appeal to Popular Opinion* (University Park, PA: Penn State University Press, 1999). For the *ad baculum*, good sources are the paper by John Woods ('Appeal to Force," in *Fallacies: Classical and Contemporary Readings*, edited by Hans V. Hansen and Robert C. Pinto, University Park, PA: Penn State University Press, 1995), pp. 240–250, and Douglas Walton's *Scare Tactics: Arguments That Appeal to Fear and Threats* (Dordrecht: Kluwer Academic, 2000).

CHAPTER 7

The *Ad Verecundiam* and the Misuse of Experts

1 Introduction

The last two chapters have concentrated on *'ad'* arguments, appeals to components of our experience that offer to support a variety of claims. One further *'ad'* argument that deserves fuller study is *ad verecundiam*, or the Appeal to Authority or Expertise.

The Appeal to Authority is a strategy in argument that few can avoid making. When my doctor tells me that I must make some serious lifestyle changes or else expect undesirable consequences to follow, then my deliberations in deciding whether to make such adjustments involve a direct appeal to her status as an authority. She has knowledge that I do not possess, coupled with many years of experience reviewing the symptoms of people comparable to me. In principle, I could acquire this knowledge and experience directly, but it is simply not practical for me to enter medical school and subsequent practice as a family physician. In the absence of the direct evidence that it is not practical for me to acquire, I rely on the testimony of an expert. Similar situations govern a wide range of my interactions with people or sources that are judged authorities of some description. In the extremely complex world in which we live, no one can be expected to be knowledgeable about everything that affects him and so we must necessarily rely on and trust the say-so of other people. The issue is deciding when that trust is well placed and when it is not. And this holds as much in our professional lives as in the day-to-day reasoning we conduct outside them. Consider, for example, the way teams of scientists conduct their work. Invariably, they build on the work of previous teams in their own and related fields. They accept the results of others' experiments and sometimes the conclusions inferred from those results. It would be impractical and often impossible for the teams to replicate all the experiments on which they rely. Hence, they accept them on the authority or expertise of those who conducted them, assuming they have been conducted according to professional standards and procedures.

When consulting a physician or mechanic, I do not think that my subsequent deliberations are fallacious. Yet the 'Appeal to Authority' has regularly been dismissed as a fallacy. Seeing why this is so requires us to explore this argument type in more detail and consider the various ways in which it arises.

2 Authorities and Experts

In Locke's original treatment of the *argumentum ad verecundiam*, he points out that people may draw on someone of eminence, using that person's word as backing for a claim. This gives weight or power to the argument because the audience, feeling an appropriate awe in the face of such an eminent authority, would be ashamed to challenge that person's word and hence is led to accept the argument. Locke suggests that there is something problematic about this persuasive move, and he is right to do so. There is something clearly coercive going on in this description.

Locke is vague, though, in regard to the nature of the authority involved. His description involves more than just knowledge; it includes, for instance, prestige and fame, which could derive from many sources. We can imagine, for example, how social standing would have carried more weight in Locke's time (the late 1600s) than it might today. What Locke may have in mind here is the way people would defer to others who were thought to have greater status. A clear example is the way scholars in the mediaeval world deferred to the authority of Aristotle.[1] We can also think about the kind of authority that would have been exercised by a sovereign or person who had political power. His saying something would be a reason for acting on the assumption that it was the case, even if it was not a reason for believing it.

This is clearly one *type* of authority that we must consider when discussing the *ad verecundiam*. We might call this the 'argument *of* authority', which stems from the particular position a person holds. Modern treatments, however, tend to stress the cognitive element in authority arguments and restrict the *ad verecundiam* to arguments that draw on authorities for specific kinds of knowledge that it is not possible to provide in any other way, such as the appeal to the physician detailed earlier. Here, the person has eminence by virtue of possessing a type of expertise that is not generally available. Modern Appeals to Authorities, then, may often be Appeals to Experts. One source of fallacy is suggested here. It may be possible for an audience to mistake a person's status as an authoritative figure for expertise in a field. When only the first exists but the second is understood, then error could arise. In following modern treatments, we will restrict our attention to the knowledge claims of experts, while being alert to the possibility of the error just noted. A person or source is in a position of expertise

---

[1] You might be inclined to think that we have been doing something similar in this book, often giving prominence to Aristotle's early treatments of fallacies he was the first to identify. But we have also noted and provided serious critical evaluation of his ideas, and this would set such discussions apart from the way mediaeval scholars seemed to defer repeatedly to Aristotle's word on a subject.

if her position in a field of knowledge is such that her pronouncements are likely to have a higher rate of success or accuracy than
those of a nonexpert.[2]

3 Testimony

Also related to this argumentative strategy is the question of testimony generally. The word of an authority or expert is a type of
testimony, and testimony is one of the principal sources for the
beliefs we hold. Reports gathered from others, along with percep-
tion, memory, and inference, contribute to what we know about
the world and each other. When we talk about whether something
conforms to experience *in general*, we are appealing to what we
have come to accept of how other people experience the world.
Then when we review what particular individuals tell us, we are
comparing that to what we know about the world. Really, we are
comparing testimony with testimony, assuming that that which is
based on wide experience is more reliable.

In argumentation we are often asked to accept a range of claims
on the basis of someone's testimony. Claims about an individual's
state of mind or specific experiences, for example, will be accepted
simply on the basis of her saying so. Another of Grice's maxims for
communication is that of Honesty, whereby we expect people to
be honest if they want to communicate. So, unless we have some
reason to doubt their trustworthiness in the reports they give, there
is always a presumption in favour of claims based on a person's
testimony. We doubt testimonies when they fall outside common
experience or are contradicted by the weight of other evidence.
They are, then, while necessary to us in forming many beliefs, a
weaker kind of evidence: they give us reliable information about an
individual, but as soon as we move to a wider arena, they provide
little by way of compelling evidence.

[2] John Woods and Douglas Walton, *Fallacies: Selected Papers 1972–1982* (Dordrecht:
Foris, 1989), p. 15.

4 | The General Appeal to an Expert

The exception to the rule just suggested occurs when we are dealing with people whose testimony is characterized by expertise. Such people have a particular claim to our consideration because their experience stands above general experience in important ways. When arguers appeal to such people, provided that their arguments meet the correct criteria that we will discuss later, we have grounds to accept the claims they support.

Starkly presented, the argument in question states

Someone (or some source) asserts a statement S.
Therefore, S is true.

Attempts have been made to construe both formal and nonformal versions of this strategy. Hamblin,[3] for example, considers

Everything X says is true.
X says that P.
Therefore P.

The crucial premise here is the first one, which renders the argument form valid. But unless that premise is an appeal to a divine being, it claims too much, and certainly more than could be verified. In fact, implicit in that premise are many of the problems that we will see associated with the Appeal to Authority that so often result in its fallaciousness. Consider an example.

Case 7A

Everything the president says is true.
The president says that Iraq has weapons of mass destruction.
Therefore, Iraq has weapons of mass destruction.

This is obviously a controversial example. But for our purposes here the statement deserving most attention is the one offered as

---

[3] Charles L. Hamblin, *Fallacies* (London: Methuen, 1970), p. 218.

the first premise. Given what we know about human beings generally, it stretches belief to imagine that someone could always be correct in his or her pronouncements. But we need to consider what exactly is wrong here beyond this questionable plausibility. Would someone be misled by such a claim? Locke's original treatment of the *ad verecundiam* suggests that someone might, because he may have such a high regard for the office of the president, so as to be inclined to give the holder of that office the benefit of the doubt. That is, he would be ashamed to challenge the word of the president because of who he is, believing perhaps that all claims he would make were the result of intelligence gathering that would justify them. And Locke's implied reservations about this strategy show what is wrong here, because the first premise appears as an attempt to immunize the argument from criticism. Presented in a dialogue, for example, it would have the effect of preventing any critical challenge in advance and so impeding the progress of the dialogue.

Those who judge the Appeal to Authority as always fallacious would focus on just this kind of example. But other ways of phrasing the general appeal show it to be more complex. Salmon,[4] for example, offers an inductively correct version of the strategy as follows:

> The vast majority of statements made by E concerning subject S are true.
> A is a statement made by E concerning subject S.
> Therefore, A is true.

This at least gives probable grounds for the conclusion asserted while it allows that any particular assertion by the expert could be wrong. It still leaves a range of contextual questions to be asked relating to the expert in question, the subject area involved, and

---

[4] Wesley Salmon, *Logic* (Englewood Cliffs, NJ: Prentice-Hall, 1963), p. 64.

what has been stated on the occasion in question. Consider an example that fits this pattern:

Case 7B

The vast majority of statements made by the singer Bono concerning AIDS in Africa are true.

Bono said AIDS in·Africa is the worst pandemic in 600 years.

Therefore, AIDS in Africa is the worst pandemic in 600 years.

The first premise here avoids the fault of that in the previous example and would allow for a dialectical exchange in which a critic challenged the word of the authority. But this example points to some of the more complex issues that will occupy us later in the chapter. What constitutes an expert in this particular subject area and how does a popular singer qualify? Is AIDS in Africa a clear field of expertise that has a body of knowledge associated with it such that we can speak of experts? And does Bono have a vested interest here such that it benefits him to associate with a high-profile health issue? These questions warrant a more detailed assessment of the appeal to authority and a range of associated critical questions. But for now we can consider some very basic Critical Questions that can help us deal with the general types of appeal.

Critical Questions

1. Is the proposed person or source a genuine authority?
2. Did the authority make the attributed claim?
3. Are the authority and claim made relevant to the subject matter?

The first question here is the kind of identification inquiry that we need to make to ensure that we are dealing with the cognitive kind of authority associated with expertise rather than authority stemming from an office held. Of course, it is possible that an individual or source could hold both types, but we want to exclude cases in which there is no cognitive claim at all, cases that are of the 'Argument of Authority' variety. A person or source that is a genuine authority will have credentials that support expertise in a recognized field of knowledge for which expertise is appropriate. When an arguer appeals to status only as if it constitutes expertise, then our analysis will likely bring to light a fallacious appeal.

The second question is a burden of proof question. Authorities of the expert variety sometimes have claims attributed to them that they have not made or that they have not intended in the way they have been interpreted. As laypeople or nonexperts, we will rarely have immediate access to the sources involved, so the arguer has a burden of proof either to provide support for the claim that an expert has said something or to give the means by which a critical appraiser could investigate the source. The latter is usually done by providing a clear reference to the place or source where the expert's pronouncement can be found.

Finally, the third question allows for cases in which a recognized expert is appealed to in support of a claim for which the expertise is not strictly relevant. A criminal psychologist, for example, has a clear claim to expertise in a range of related subject matters but would not obviously have any relevant contribution *as a criminal psychologist* to a debate over the morality of capital punishment. In such an area, the expert's statements are likely to have no stronger standing than those of the nonexpert, unless a relevant relationship can be shown by the arguer.

5   Ways of Fallaciousness: Complexities of the Appeal

As we will proceed to see, appeals to the authority of experts involve greater complexities than these three questions bring to light, but in many cases they may be sufficient to allow us to deal adequately with arguments and identify fallaciousness. A fuller treatment will involve several considerations.

The skepticism we have toward claims based on testimony, when these claims exceed personal experience, may account for the skepticism that is also directed toward claims based on the authority of expertise. After all, what is often at stake is the expert's own personal experience, and what many of these appeals reduce to is a conflict between different testimonies or experiences. If we are to accept that some people's testimonies count for more than those of others, we need to have criteria for judging these. What are needed are clear conditions that allow us to distinguish the legitimate appeals from those that are fallacious. What follow are six considerations crucial to deciding the presence of fallacious appeals to experts and a seventh one that can also prove useful. These will serve as our Critical Questions for assessing examples of the *ad verecundiam* argument.

Critical Questions

1. The authority or expert (whether a person, institution, or source) must be identified and should have a track record that increases the reliability of the statements over related statements from sources that do not possess the expertise. Appeals to unidentified experts with unknown or weak track records can be judged fallacious.

2. The authority should be in a field that lends itself to expert knowledge. That is, it should constitute a body of knowledge over which it would be appropriate for someone to have expertise. Failure to meet this condition will result in a fallacious appeal.

3. The expert's statements must be both related to the field of expertise and relevant to the question at hand. This is the relevance question seen earlier.

4. Direct knowledge could be acquired by the person making the appeal, at least in principle. That is, there must be some way of testing or verifying the expert's claims.

5. The expert should not have a vested interest in the claim so as to benefit from the outcome. Where such illegitimate bias is clear or suggested, the appeal is weakened to the point of being fallacious.

6. We would prefer that there be some consensus in the field – or, where this does not exist, as with conflicting expert witnesses in a trial, that the claims are consistent with other knowledge within the relevant field.

7. Claims with more serious consequences should be given greater weight than those with less.

We will explore each of these in turn and consider them in light of some constructed examples. For the most part, they are not simple to apply and will require sensitivity to various examples.

1. *The identity question*: Who or what is the source of expertise appealed to and what are the credentials and track record? If we are going to treat appeals to experts as serious types of 'testimony arguments', there must be something that distinguishes them from general testimony about the world. Experts such as scientists or polling companies or government agencies need to be clearly identified by name so that someone could in principle follow up by researching the source. Appeals to experts are, after all, sorts of promissory reasons in support of claims. They promise that the evidence is available but is perhaps too difficult to present in the argument. The name of the expert person or source stands as a kind of guarantor that the evidence does exist somewhere. But for this to be credible, specific identifiable information about the expert source must be provided along with something that makes us believe that expert is reliable. The track record or standing in the field (often represented by the credentials earned) is good support for that credibility. There should be enough information to allow

an interested party to go beyond the guarantee of the authority argument to verify what has been said.

Case 7C

Recent scientific studies have linked the sweetener Aspartame to cancers in laboratory animals. Given the prevalence of Aspartame in diet drinks, it should be removed from the market.

The conclusion to be supported may well be one with which we have sympathy. But the question here is whether we have good grounds for believing the conclusion on the basis of the authority claim provided. And we do not. The only evidence for the advocated removal are 'recent scientific studies', but unidentified studies cannot be corroborated or verified and so the appeal to them is fallacious. This is what is sometimes called hear-say evidence in law courts, and judges are disinclined to accept it for the reasons we have noted. An obvious problem arises in the serious cases of whistleblowing, in which an arguer has good reason to protect the identity of a source. But as evidence in an argument such appeals are at best weak and largely worthless. This is why institutions take pains in establishing policies that will protect whistleblowers once they have been identified.

2. *The field question*: What constitutes a body of knowledge such that we can feel confident there could be experts in that field? This is a difficult question, not least because new areas of knowledge develop over time and it is often a matter of some debate whether and when they have gained credibility. Consider Web technology, human cloning, modern warfare, and clinical ecology. Take the last of these as an example. This 'field' contains scientists who have excellent credentials who believe that chemicals and environmental pollutants cause a range of human ailments.[5] The problem is that there is massive disagreement within the field, and other

---

[5] Douglas Walton, *Appeal to Expert Opinion: Arguments from Authority* (University Park, PA: Penn State University Press, 1997), p. 176.

scientists outside it do not consider the field itself legitimate. In most instances, laypeople will have no difficulty in recognizing established fields with experts, but in the case of new and developing fields we may have no other option than to judge appeals weak and look for other kinds of evidence to support claims.

Case 7D

It is remarkable that people would still doubt that the Earth has been visited by extraterrestrials in the distant past. Erich von Däniken, the world's most successful non-fiction writer of all time, has written 26 books on the topic and has sold over 63 million copies worldwide.

This case illustrates the concern covered by question 2. An expert is appealed to in support of the implicit claim that the Earth has been visited by extraterrestrials, and we are given something of his credentials. But we might have serious doubts whether this constitutes a field with a body of knowledge, especially knowledge derived from sources other than books written by von Däniken. One thing we would require of such a field is general acceptance of it, but that would not seem present in such a controversial case. It may be that we have here a field in its infancy that will gain general acceptance in time. But at this point, the evidence tells against it and we must judge this appeal to be fallacious.

3. *The relevance question*: This requires that the expert be speaking in her or his field of expertise and that what is said is relevant to the claim being advanced. In terms of our interest in ways people may be misled by fallacious arguments, it is not difficult to imagine that someone who is impressed by the clear standing that an expert has in a field could overlook the fact that he or she is not pronouncing on something related to that field. Consider how often recognized experts write to newspapers, remarking on some important issue of the day as if their expertise in, say, evolutionary theory could be transferred to the religious causes of global terrorism.

Case 7E

Dr. Spock said that "no human, no child, no adult needs cow's milk–it's a deception on the government's part to promote." So, don't listen to me. Take the advice of Dr. Spock, arguably the most influential pediatrician of all time.

Dr. Spock was and is still an outstanding expert in the field of pediatrics and child-rearing, and he did make the remark attributed to him here. But he also said many strange things toward the end of his long life and this could be one of them. There is a dispute about the pros and cons of drinking milk. But is this a dispute in which Spock's word would be valuable given his particular area of expertise? His remark does include children, but it goes beyond this to cover adults and offer commentary on the government's behaviour. His expert status as pediatrician does not obviously extend to these other aspects of the issue around the effects of drinking milk, and so this appears to be a strong candidate for a fallacious Appeal to Authority.

4. *The testability question*: This recognizes the promissory nature of Appeals to Authority and ensures that there is some way to follow up on what the authority is saying or what is being attributed to him. If there is no way in principle to verify what is being claimed, then this must weaken the authority claim because it brings into question the grounds for holding it. Covered by this question would be cases in which we judge that the authority is offering an opinion or speculating, rather than providing a claim that is directly related to what she knows.

Case 7F

Out of Body Experiences (OBEs) have been given a considerable boost since the experiment reported in 1980 by Osis and McCormick. The subject of the experiment was a psychic, Alex Tanous, who induced OBEs during which he identified remote targets that could normally only be viewed from a very specific location.

This case could also fail under the requirements of question 2, since it is a matter of debate whether we have experts in fields of psychic phenomena. But here the larger problem lies in the way such information provided by Tanous could be verified to confirm that it is evidence of an OBE, rather than something else. Tanous appears to have related his direct experience, but there is no way by which to confirm this, and this is a case in which the alleged direct experience conflicts with common experience.

5. *The bias question*: This is another serious one that will often be a key reason why an Appeal to Authority is judged fallacious. Biases can take a number of forms and need not always be illegitimate. After all, if we are open about our biases and they stem from real associations and beliefs that we hold, then there is no reason why they should interfere with the way we reason. But when we are dealing with authorities and credibility it does certainly matter whether someone has an illegitimate bias in the form of some vested interest such that she stands to gain in some way from the case in question. Celebrities, for example, are effective in promoting products and services because of the way people like to associate with them. But even when they are promoting things that relate to their field of knowledge (that is, where they might pass question 1), they are undermined as authorities because they stand to gain insofar as they are being paid to say what they say. If we hire a consultant to research and offer advice on the best area of a city to locate our new business, then it makes sense to take that advice. But if our consultant then offers to sell us property in that area of the city, we may question the initial advice since the consultant now seems to have had a further interest in our decision.

Case 7G

The claims that second-hand smoke represents a serious health risk to people are wildly overstated. Consider, for example, a recent study (in the May 17, 2003 issue of the *British Medical Journal*) conducted by a team of researchers from the UCLA School of Public Health. Lead investigator Dr. James Enstrom reported "We found no measurable effect from being exposed to secondhand smoke and an increased risk of heart disease or lung cancer in nonsmokers."

This appears to be a bona fide appeal to an expert. We have a source clearly identified (both the researcher and the medium in which the research is reported) and what is stated is relevant to the field of expertise. But because the expert is identified and the source clearly cited, we are able to follow up and do our own research. This brings to light some of the counterargumentation from the American Cancer Society, which notes that the study was funded in part by the Center for Indoor Air Research, which is an arm of Philip Morris and other tobacco companies. Dr. Enstrom had requested and received funding in 1997. It is possible that the research conclusion is well founded, but the vested interest through the association with the tobacco companies shows the Appeal to Authority argument to be a fallacious one.[6]

6. *The consensus question*: This is another one that has to be weighed carefully. The fact that experts disagree does not mean that none of them is correct. It does mean that it is much harder for us to appreciate who is correct. The culture of parading experts on both sides of an issue through courtrooms has made this quite clear. There are also mavericks in a field who discover things far ahead of everyone else and have a hard time establishing what later becomes a widely accepted view (consider the cases of a Freud or a Darwin). But where there is a clear consensus in a field and someone appeals to an expert who makes a claim contrary to that consensus, we have no other option than to conclude that, in this case, we do not have

[6] It should be noted that the ACS has used the strategy of Guilt by Association in its counterargumentation. But insofar as the association does exist and is relevant to the question of whether the findings are reliable, then the argument is not a fallacious variety of that strategy.

grounds for a good Appeal to Authority argument. And we must judge the appeal fallacious.

Case 7H

We should be very wary of rushing forward with the Kyoto agreement on climate change. The case for human-caused climate change and global warming is still to be made to a degree that would warrant us seriously changing our behaviour. After all, the *Wall Street Journal* editors note (June 21, 2005) that "the scientific case . . . looks weaker all the time" and that "Since that Byrd-Hagel vote eight years ago, the case for linking fossil fuels to global warming has, if anything, become even more doubtful."

Again, we have an Appeal to Authority here (the *Wall Street Journal* editors) that appears to meet many of the critical questions we have been considering. But any acquaintance with positions on this issue would reveal that this opinion flies in the face of other views. As critics quickly pointed out, just a week earlier the U.S. National Academy of Sciences and ten other leading world bodies agreed that there was significant evidence in support of global warming, and that it was likely that most recent warming could be attributed to human activities. In short, not only is there no consensus supporting the expert opinion expressed in the argument, the consensus would actually appear to oppose it. Hence, we have another fallacious appeal.

7. The final question is not strictly a fallacy identifier, but it is a useful consideration when weighing arguments from authority. This question is *the consequences question*. What are the consequences of accepting what the authority says, or ignoring what is said? In practical circumstances, where we weigh the difficult considerations brought to light by the other six questions, this consideration of consequences may well become a deciding factor in whether we accept an argument from authority that has not been revealed as clearly fallacious. After all, if I choose not to believe

that extraterrestrials visited the Earth in the distant past or that OBEs occur, that disbelief will likely have little impact on my daily affairs or future. But if I ignore the advice of a medical expert who suggests I need to make some adjustments to my lifestyle, then that disbelief could have a serious impact on both my daily affairs and future.

6 | Summary

The foregoing will indicate the central issues when dealing with authority arguments and gauging their fallaciousness. It should be clear just how complex these arguments can be and how very dependent they are on contextual factors. In several of the cases used to illustrate points the problems are detected only because we have wider knowledge of an issue that can make us suspicious of some expert claims. The *ad verecundiam*, as its early expression by Locke indicated, is very much an argument in which the strengths and weaknesses are external to the propositions involved, lying in the contextual factors surrounding an issue. This draws attention to what Charles Willard[7] has called *the* problem of authority and our dependence on it for much of our information. The complexity of the issues for which we need and rely on authorities encourages that reliance to the extent that we start to lose our autonomy. Mistrust in the argument from authority is often phrased in just these terms because we are letting other people think for us when we should try always to reason for ourselves, to be autonomous (self-governed) in our thinking. This creates a dilemma for us: we must balance our dependency on the testimony of experts in public and personal decision making with the development of our own competence as critical thinkers. This observation further explains how people can so easily succumb to fallacious appeals to authorities.

[7] Charles A. Willard, "Authority," *Informal Logic* 12 (1990), pp. 11–22.

Insofar as we cannot avoid our twenty-first-century dependence on authorities we must protect our autonomy by developing our competence in dealing with them, learning to appraise authority arguments, and recognizing when appeals are fallacious. The details of this chapter should assist you in that endeavour.

CHAPTER EXERCISES

In the following passages, decide when Appeals to Authority are being used and appraise those arguments for fallaciousness. Remember, we are looking not simply for the mention of an authority, but for a direct appeal to the authority, a *use* of an expert to support a claim.

1. This piece is from an article that responded to concerns after media reports in 1988 that a scientist, Dr. Richard Steed, announced that he planned to open a cloning clinic in every suburban mall:

   Reproductive scientists are agreed that it will be years before anyone can safely clone human beings. Thus, there is ample time for informed public debate.

2. Television ad:

   My life is about writing my own script. That's why my card is American Express. (Ellen DeGeneres, actress)

3. According to the noted scientist Richard Dawkins in *The Devil's Chaplain*, religion is "the most inflammatory enemy-labelling device in history" (p. 159). Even Hitler's beliefs were a religion of his own making. So religion is not the positive influence on society that we have been led to believe.

4. From an advertisement for Gillette's Mach, accompanied by a picture of the soccer star David Beckham, accessed August 5, 2005, http://www.gillettem3power.com/beckham/:

Grooming Tips: There's only one David Beckham, but anyone can look and feel their best by following these Gillette tips used by the master midfielder himself. Tip 1: Always soak before you shave. Start by washing your face and neck with warm water and a mild soap. This will remove natural oils and perspiration that can build up (especially after a tough day on the field), making it difficult for your skin to absorb water. After about three minutes of soaking, your beard hair will be optimally softened for an easier shave. [Seven other tips follow.]

5. From J. Savage, *Evolution* (New York: Holt, Rinehart, & Winston, 1965), Preface:

   No serious biologist today doubts the fact of evolution.... The fact of evolution is amply clear. We do not need a listing of evidences to demonstrate the fact of evolution any more than we need to demonstrate the existence of mountain ranges.

6. I have heard it repeated that very little in our technical fields of biology makes sense unless viewed in light of the theory of evolution. This neo-Darwinist humbug has been exposed as such by a document posted on the Internet by 150 scientists named "A Scientific Dissent from Darwinism," which states: "We are skeptical of claims for the ability of random mutations and natural selection to account for the complexity of life. Careful examination of the evidence for Darwinian theory should be encouraged."

7. From an article on Arianna Online, June 19, 2003, accessed June 22, 2004, http://www.workingforchange.com/article.cfm?itemid= 15180&CFID=8038824&CFTOKEN=59982221:

   By all accounts, the behind-the-scenes battle within the Bush administration over just what information should be used, or spun, or hidden, to make the case that Saddam Hussein posed an imminent threat to America and the rest of the world was a knockdown, drag-out fight between the facts and a zealous, highly politicized, "who needs proof?" mindset. And, at the end of the day, the truth was left writhing on the floor.

Hey, why let the facts get in the way of a perfectly good war?

This pathological pattern of disregarding inconvenient reality is not just troubling – it's deadly. And it's threatening to drag us into a Sisyphean struggle against evildoers in Syria, Iran, North Korea, or whatever locale Karl Rove thinks would best advance "Operation Avoid 41's Fate."

Since I'm not a psychiatrist, I consulted the work of various experts in the field in order to get a better understanding of the fanatical mind-set that is driving the Bush administration's agenda – and scaring the living daylights out of a growing number of observers. Dr. Norman Doidge, professor of psychiatry at the University of Toronto, has identified among the telltale symptoms of fanatics: an intolerance of dissent, a doctrine that is riddled with contradictions, the belief that one's cause has been blessed or even commanded by God, and the use of reinforcement techniques such as repetition to spread one's message. Sound like anyone you know?

8. A letter to the editor, *New York Times*, July 1, 2004, accessed July 1, 2004, http://www.nytimes.com/2004/07/01/opinion/L01ENEM.html:

I find the idea that enemy soldiers and terrorists have standing in American courts ridiculous.

Abraham Lincoln, considered one of the greatest presidents, suspended the writ of habeas corpus when it suited him, held "enemy combatants" indefinitely without trial and violated the First Amendment by shutting down newspapers that published articles he considered not in the national interest.

I am not sure I see a difference in the actions of the two presidents, except that President Bush hasn't gone nearly as far as Lincoln did.

9. Background: In the winter of 2005, Ann Veneman was nominated to serve as the executive director of the United Nations Children's Fund (UNICEF). Several people objected. Part of the case made against Ms. Veneman (constructed from news reports) is as follows:

Ms. Veneman's training and experience as a corporate lawyer for agribusiness do not qualify her for the substantial task of leading the agency most responsible for the rights of children worldwide. There is no evidence in her tenure as U.S. secretary of agriculture, secretary of the California Department of Food and Agriculture, or deputy undersecretary for international affairs of the USDA of her interest in the world's children or their health and well-being. Indeed, her performance in these positions has been characterized by the elevation of corporate profit above people's right to food (U.N. Declaration of Human Rights, Article 25). Such a philosophy and practice would reverse almost six decades of UNICEF's proud humanitarian history and prove disastrous for the world's children. Veneman's corporate sympathies will conflict with her duty to protect children. She should not serve as the next executive director of UNICEF.

10. From "Why the Catholic Church Maintains a Male Priesthood" by G. Emmett Cardinal Carter, archbishop emeritus of Toronto, *Globe and Mail*, April 7, 1997:

The dignity and rights of women are at the heart of contemporary Catholic social teaching. One need only read the Pope's 1988 *Apostolic Letter on the Dignity and Vocation of Women* or his remarkable 1995 letter to women on the occasion of the United Nations World Conference on Women in Beijing. In the latter he expresses his gratitude to women for their contributions in home, church and society. He condemns all forms of prejudice and violence against women. While recognizing positive achievements of the women's movement, he calls for a renewed effort to overcome discrimination and injustice through "an effective and intelligent campaign for the promotion of women, concentrating on all areas of women's life and beginning with a universal recognition of the dignity of women."

FURTHER READING

Some interesting theoretical issues emerge in this chapter, and each of them will reward further study. Issues surrounding the questions of testimony are taken up in C. A. J. Coady, *Testimony: A Philosophical Study* (Oxford: Clarendon Press, 1992), and problems related specifically to authority are addressed in Charles A. Willard, "Authority," *Informal Logic* 12 (1990), pp. 11–22. Both topics are explored in more detail in Christopher W. Tindale, "The Authority of Testimony," *Protosociology: An International Journal of Interdisciplinary Research* 13 (1999), pp. 96–116. A good source to study further the relationship between good and fallacious examples of the argument scheme is Douglas Walton, *Appeal to Expert Opinion: Arguments from Authority* (University Park, PA: Penn State Press, 1997).

CHAPTER 8

Sampling

1 Introduction

As some of our earlier discussions have indicated, one major variety of reasoning in which we engage is inductive reasoning, whereby a conclusion is drawn on the basis of experience that is in some way incomplete. We decide that something will be a certain way because we, and perhaps others, have found it to be that way in the past. What we are drawing from for our evidence is what we take to be a representative sample of cases of the thing in question. The better the sample, or range and depth of experience, the more justified is the conclusion drawn from it. The most public way in which we see this kind of reasoning is through the reported results of opinion polls.

As early as the *Port Royal Logic* (1662)[1] logicians have identified invalid inductions as a species of fallacy. Inductions based on fewer than all instances, we are told, often lead us into error.

---

[1] The most readily available edition of the 1662 *Logic* is Antoine Arnauld and Pierre Nicole, *Antoine Arnauld and Pierre Nicole: Logic and the Art of Thinking*, edited by Jill Vance Buroker (Cambridge: Cambridge University Press, 1996).

But we inevitably have to reason on the basis of fewer than all instances, so the opportunities for error are extensive. The question is how few instances we can accept before the conclusion we draw is unjustified, and the answer will depend on the contexts involved and the types of things we are reasoning about. The fallacy that arises when we conclude too much on too little evidence has come to be called the Hasty Generalization.

Another variety of problem with generalizations is that we may fail to recognize appropriate exceptions. The fallacy involved here is called *secundum quid*, and again this has a long history.

In this chapter, we will explore first the nature of generalizations and the kinds of problems that arise with them before proceeding to consider the various ways in which fallacies arise in the sampling and measurement errors associated with polls.

2 Generalizations

A generalization applies some property to a group of things rather than some particular thing. As Douglas Walton[2] has explained, there are different kinds of generalization. Some generalizations are absolute or universal: whatever property is being generalized applies to every member of the group without exception. 'All crows are black' is such a generalization insofar as it attributes the property of being black to every crow; there are no nonblack crows. Of course, absolute generalizations such as this may be particularly susceptible to counterinstances, and arguers have to be sure when they use such statements that they do refer to every member. "No member of my party would ever be involved in any behavior that might bring the party into disrepute" is the kind of confident

---

[2] Douglas Walton, *Fundamentals of Critical Argumentation* (Cambridge: Cambridge University Press, 2006), p. 15.

statement we often see issued by a political leader, only to have it contradicted by a subsequent investigation.

Another category of generalization is the inductive generalization, which asserts that a property holds in a group to a specific extent, but not universally. 'Most politicians are committed to responsible environmental policies' is a generalization that allows for exceptions and so is not vulnerable to the counterexample in the way that a universal generalization is. But we still need to look carefully at the sample of politicians that has been examined to support this assertion and so gauge the probability that it is correct. When a specific number is attached to the membership that has a property, as we see in poll results, then the inductive generalization is a statistical one: '77 percent of Americans support the president's economic program' fits this description.

An important kind of nonabsolute generalization discussed by Walton (pp. 17–18) is the presumptive defeasible generalization. This type tells us that some members of a group generally have a certain property. 'Birds fly' illustrates this kind of generalization. Such a statement tells us what the case is typically but does not overcommit us so that we are defeated when people point to various kinds of birds that do not fly. As opposed to the strictness of the universal generalizations, these are the weakest kind. A key difference between inductive and defeasible generalizations is the ability to calculate the likely number of instances in the first case. Defeasible generalizations are so weak that this is not possible, and thus prediction becomes more difficult. Hence there are dangers in using defeasible generalizations that may not occur with the others. It may be easier to overgeneralize and make Hasty Generalizations. This would also suggest that people may be more likely to commit this kind of error, led by the imprecision associated with such statements to conclude more than is warranted by the evidence. As we will see, we are in particular danger of overlooking exceptions when dealing with defeasible generalizations.

Hasty Generalizations

As Hamblin points out,[3] the difficulty in dealing with inductive fallacies of the kind we envisage here is that of distinguishing between good and bad inductions. While the *Port Royal* is correct in warning us that 'fewer than all instances' often lead us into error, they also often do not. Hamblin despairs of treating inductive shortcomings as varieties of fallacy, but we cannot afford to be so generous when problematic instances plainly assail us. Consider the following case:

Case 8A

This is a letter to *The Independent*, August 10, 2004. The letter itself establishes the background we need; the M25 is a motorway around London.

Sir: Yasmin Alibhai-Brown falls into two traps in her column "We're becoming an awful place to visit" (9 August). Firstly, she talks about London as if it is Britain. It isn't (although as a journalist, Ms Alibhai-Brown would not necessarily know). As a Londoner, I am constantly surprised by how nice people are in other parts of Britain. I equally find myself asking why people become such ogres once they are within the M25 perimeter. The same goes for Parisians and the French, New Yorkers and Americans, and so on. Clearly cities are not the place to see human beings at their best.

There are several interesting things to note in this case. To begin with, the writer accuses Alibhai-Brown of generalizing about Britain on the basis of what she knows about London. But then the writer proceeds to generalize himself. As a Londoner, he finds

---

[3] Charles L. Hamblin, *Fallacie* (London: Methuen, 1970), p. 47.

people friendly in other parts of Britain but "ogres" within the London perimeter. Presumably, he is not suggesting a universal generalization, that 'all Londoners are ogres (or unfriendly)', but is offering a defeasible generalization about what is typically the case. The immediate thing to note about this is that it is based on his experience, and we do not know whether his experience is representative. But he goes further in his reasoning, drawing a strong ("Clearly") conclusion about cities: "cities are not the place to see human beings at their best."

Again, it is charitable to read this as a defeasible claim. But what is his evidence for the claim? To the instance of Londoners (drawn from his experience) he adds those of "Parisians and the French, New Yorkers and Americans." The grounds for these defeasible generalizations are unclear, but he is using these three cities to support a conclusion about cities generally.

Hamblin's warning, together with the remarks drawn from Walton's discussion, make clear that it is difficult to determine how many cities *would* be required to support a claim about cities 'generally'. But that does not mean we cannot judge cases in which the evidence is obviously insufficient. Given the large number of cities in the world, even cities on the scale of a London or New York, it is apparent that three is not enough evidence to support a generalization of this kind adequately. Hence, we have a fallacy of Hasty Generalization in the move from three instances of a group to the claim about that group generally.

Also, as we saw in the previous chapter, testimony drawn from experience has a powerful hold over us, and our own experience is particularly immediate. It is not surprising that we should draw on the assumption that our own experience is typical, and this helps explain how we might come to commit such errors. But as a case such as this illustrates, we must be more objective about the way we argue from our own experience and be prepared to face a burden of proof to support why it should be taken as typical. That does not happen here and so the inference from the arguer's experience to the claim about Londoners' being generally unfriendly also commits the fallacy of Hasty Generalization.

Given that there is no preordained number of cases required for a good induction, each case must be reviewed according to its own merits. Depending on what it is that is being generalized (crows, cities) and the information available, we will need to make a case for our judgment that the evidence is sufficient or insufficient, and hence the presence of a Hasty Generalization in the case of the latter.

Secundum Quid

As Walton points out (p. 20), a problem that arises with arguments based on generalization is that "some people who are passionately committed to a viewpoint tend to overlook qualifications that are needed in a specific case." Showing someone who holds to absolutes that exceptions may be warranted can be one of the more difficult tasks we take on as arguers. The type of Hasty Generalization captured in this error is called the *secundum quid*.[4] Traditionally, this has been the term used for all Hasty Generalizations, but modern treatments have drawn the distinction between the hasty inductions of the last section and the failure to accommodate relevant exceptions. It is the latter that interests us here. *Secundum quid* means "in a certain respect" and refers to qualifications that may be attached to a generalization. What is the case in a certain respect may not hold generally. Sometimes a close association to an issue or perspective may blind us to reasonable exceptions to a general rule.

---

[4] A further name applied to this fallacy is 'Sweeping Generalization' because it involves applying a general rule to a case to which it is not applicable. S. Morris Engel, *With Good Reason*, 4th ed. (New York: St. Martin's Press, 1994), pp. 133–136.

Case 8B

People should be allowed to do whatever they want.

Smith wants to go over Niagara Falls in a barrel.

Therefore, Smith should be allowed to go over Niagara Falls in a barrel.

The first premise is a general principle that is widely accepted. The problem occurs when we try to apply it to someone who is an exception to the rule. Someone who has self-destructive tendencies would seem to be a person who should be restrained from doing *everything* he wants, because it is not in his interests to do so. Normally, even as we express a statement like the first premise, we are well aware that this cannot apply universally and that there must be reasonable exceptions. The challenge lies in recognizing what counts as a reasonable exception. Again, there can be no hard-and-fast rule to help us here. Given the contextual nature of the argumentation involved, we will have to review matters on a case by case basis and present our own reasons for why we believe the fallacy has been committed.

3 Treatment of Generalization Fallacies

The Gambler's Fallacy

Our review of generalization has focused on the ways we deal with various probabilities in arguments. In fact, bad inductive arguments arise from errors made about probabilities. This leads us to some of the research done by cognitive psychologists into ways people make errors when reasoning – research related to our interests in how fallacious reasoning can arise. We can see an example of such errors in what is widely called the 'Gambler's Fallacy'. People tend to believe that the longer a series runs without a certain occurrence (hands of cards when red cards rather than black cards have been turned up, for example), then the likelihood of that occurrence increases. You may have heard people who play lotteries say something like "My numbers are bound to come up soon," and the evidence they give for this belief is the long period in which they have played the same numbers. What they fail to realize (or cannot bring themselves to accept) is that the likelihood is the same on the next draw as it was on each of the previous draws.

The work of Tversky and Kahneman into ways people make errors in reasoning may give us some insight here, and it has interested fallacy theorists for this reason. Tversky and Kahneman explained some of the errors people commit when reasoning probabilistically as due to their being led into biases by particular judgmental heuristics that they use. A heuristic is a strategy for solving a problem or making a decision. Through a series of experiments, Tversky and Kahneman were able to expose the problems related to heuristics, such as representativeness, availability, adjustment, and anchoring.[5] For example, in answering questions along the lines of whether object A belongs to class B, people typically rely on the representativeness heuristic, whereby they evaluate probabilities according to the degree by which A is representative of, or resembles, B. In terms of our present interest, this comes to light when people use this heuristic in drawing a sample from a specified population. We can present some of their findings in terms of a case:

Case 8C

A certain town is served by two hospitals. In the larger hospital about 45 babies are born each day, and in the smaller hospital about 15 babies are born each day. As you know, about 50 percent of all babies are boys.

---

[5] Amos Tversky and Daniel Kahneman, "Judgment under Uncertainty, Heuristics and Biases," in *Judgment under Uncertainty, Heuristics and Biases*, edited by D. Kahneman, P. Slovic, and A. Tversky (Cambridge: Cambridge University Press, 1982), pp. 3–20.

However, the exact percentage varies from day to day. Sometimes it may be higher than 50 percent, sometimes lower. For a period of one year, each hospital recorded the days on which more than 60 percent of the babies born were boys. Which hospital do you think recorded more such days?

The larger hospital (21)
The smaller hospital (21)
About the same (that is, within 5 percent of each other) (53)

The values in parentheses are the number of undergraduate students who chose each answer.[6]

As you can see, 53 of the subjects judged the requested probability to be the same in the small and the large hospital. This contrasts with sampling theory, which dictates that the expected number of days on which more than 60 percent of the babies born are boys is much greater in the small hospital because a large sample is less likely to stray from 50 percent. We see here a divergence between theory and people's intuition. Errors seem to arise when we are misled by judgments such as representativeness.

Critical Questions

The foregoing discussion of generalization gives us enough information to formulate the Critical Questions that will help us organize and evaluate arguments of this kind.

1. What type of generalization is being made?
2. Has the arguer concluded more than is warranted by the evidence?
3. Is this a case of a generalization that has relevant exceptions that have been missed?

---

[6] Tversky and Kahneman, "Judgment," p. 6. You should be aware that their evaluations of what is happening in such cases are far from uncontroversial. For a discussion of the debate around this issue see Gerd Gigerenzer, *Adaptive Thinking: Rationality in the Real World* (Oxford: Oxford University Press, 2000), p. 19.

The first question focuses our attention on the generalization itself and the degree to which the arguer believes it covers all cases. As we have seen, it matters what kind of inductive generalization is being expressed because we will need to assess the evidence provided in relation to the strength of the generalization.

Defeasible generalizations are weaker than inductive ones because we cannot calculate the likely number of instances. Thus while '65 percent of Britons support the prime minister's initiatives' can be assessed against available data, 'jocks are not serious students' cannot. Predictions are difficult with defeasible generalizations and the chances of error increase.

The second question requires us to weigh the evidence provided in relation to the claim made. Depending on how we answered the first question, we will be looking for different things here according to the type of generalization. We have seen that there is no set number of instances that make the support for a claim based on a generalization sufficient. We will be wary with defeasible generalizations, but with all inductions we will want to consider how many supporting instances are available and whether they are enough to make the conclusion more probable than not. Cases of clear insufficiency will stick out and make it relatively easy for us to support our charge that a fallacy of Hasty Generalization has been committed. But in other cases this will be more difficult and we will need to explain what, in our judgment, would count as sufficient support and why the argument in question falls short.

Our final question alerts us to cases of the fallacy of *secundum quid*, in which an arguer fails to accommodate what we take to be relevant exceptions to a generalization. Either he has ignored exceptions, or he has discounted them. The question here is the relevance of the exceptions. We need to show that the generalization covers cases that the arguer ignores because those cases are of the same kind.

4 | Polls and Studies

One clear source of generalizations that we cannot avoid are the surveys, polls, and studies we see reported in the media. While not obviously arguments themselves, these involve reasoning from a sample to the group generally (what is called the 'population') and so are susceptible to errors of overgeneralization. The reliability of a poll or study depends on a number of things, but principally it is important that the sample that has been surveyed or tested in some way is *representative* of the group about which a conclusion will be drawn, and that the way that sample has been measured (what is said about it) is free of bias.

A typical such piece of reasoning will involve a polling company's approaching a segment of a group (students, adult voters, pet owners) and asking questions of them ("How would you rank your educational experience?" "For whom will you vote?" "Does owning a pet enhance your quality of life?"). Then the results achieved are generalized to the entire group and deemed to be true for them. So if 60 percent of the sample questioned answer that they will vote for party A, the conclusion is drawn that 60 percent of *all* voters will vote for party A. Whether we should trust such a claim (the generalization) will depend on the nature of the sample – were enough of the right kind of people questioned? – and the clarity of what was asked of them – asking whom someone will vote for is much clearer and involves less judgment than asking whether something will enhance one's quality of life. We will look here at some of the fallacies that can arise in polling.

5 | Fallacy of Insufficient Statistics

The Fallacy of Insufficient Statistics is a type of Hasty Generalization, but one that can apply to polling samples that are not large enough. Polls are usually conducted by professional companies who employ scientific standards in their studies and evaluations. We can usually trust that pollsters have reviewed a sufficient number of the sample group to justify the generalizations *they* draw. But as these studies are picked up and reported, others (reporters, commentators) may draw their own inferences, for which the sample is not adequate. So we need to be careful to look at all the information that is available. A public opinion pollster who interviewed only 100 people could not expect to have enough evidence to support a general claim about the climate of public opinion in the nation. Cases like that, if we encounter them, will commit the Fallacy of Insufficient Statistics.

As we saw, the exact numbers that do make up a legitimate sample will vary, depending upon the population that is being studied. But the science of sampling, drawn from the laws of probability, tells us that for large groups the sample size required for a given degree of reliability increases by only small amounts as the population size increases. We saw this with the hospital example in Case 8C. People assume that an appropriate sample should be some proportion of the population, but this is wrong. Thus, you will see that the polls reported in the media generally aim for a sample of around 1,000 if they are dealing with a national survey. This may seem small for a population such as adult Americans, but it is quite sufficient. More important is that the sample is representative of the population, and this affects insufficiency if the sample has subgroups that impact the details being reported. If a poll is drawing a conclusion about all Americans that will be based on a sample of 1,000 and is then drawing further conclusions about subgroups of Americans, such as those at a certain income level or those living on the West Coast, then it is important that a sufficient number of those groups is included in the sample. Otherwise, the Fallacy of Insufficient Statistics is committed because we do not have enough of a specific subgroup to draw a reasonable conclusion about them.

6 | Fallacy of Biased Statistics

We need to distinguish the last point from cases in which there is a sample that is biased in some way so as to affect the conclusion drawn about the population (rather than about a subgroup). If we are trying to discover what students in a particular state think of the quality of college education in that state, then it is a problem if we select only students from large schools, or from professional programs, or who have low grade point averages. In each case the sample will be biased in such a way that no reliable conclusion could be drawn about students generally in that state. What might be appropriate would be a conclusion about the quality of education in large schools or certain programs, but even those depend on the full makeup of the sample. Biases become particularly prevalent in the kinds of polls run by magazines or online newspapers. An online newspaper poll asks, "Are Modern parents too involved in the lives of their teenage offspring?" and finds that an overwhelming 71 percent of respondents answer 'no' compared to 29 percent who answer 'yes'. These percentages represent 8,479 and 3,481, respectively, for a total of 11,960 respondents. This appears to be a high enough number for drawing some interesting generalizations. But the problem arises when we consider the sample in relation to any population it might represent. Online polls can be accessed from anywhere, so there is no obvious geographical limit to the data represented. Nor can we even say that this sample is representative of the newspaper's readers generally, or readers of the online edition, since we do not know what percentage of readers typically answer the poll. People self-select in responding to such questions and so, as interesting as the result seems, it tells us very little about any identifiable group. In this case, no claim is being drawn from the data, but other polls are reported as if they represent an identifiable population. When this occurs, we have an instance of the Fallacy of Biased Statistics.

There are all kinds of ways in which the sample can become biased so as to encourage a particular outcome, deliberately or otherwise. An extensively reported Harris poll (June 22, 2005) has the headline "Clear Majority of Adults Favor Bringing Most Troops Home from Iraq in Next Year." The poll found that a substantial majority of U.S. adults, by 63 to 33 percent, favored bringing most troops home. This percentage was based on a sample of 1,015 adults (aged eighteen and over) contacted by telephone within the United States between June 7 and 12, 2005. The sample was weighted for characteristics such as sex, age, race, and education to align them with their actual proportions within the population.

The most obvious suggestion of bias here arises in the way the poll was conducted, effectively selecting a sample of people at home and answering phones (we are not told whether cell phones are included). You might think about the types of people this would eliminate as potential respondents. Depending on the times of day that the calls were made, it may also rule out certain occupations. It would also seem to rule out the kind of person disinclined to answer a fairly lengthy telephone interview.

The Harris pollsters are aware of such problems, noting, after they have indicated the sampling error of the plus or minus percentage points that probability predicts for such a number as 1,015, that "there are several other sources of possible error in all polls or surveys that are probably more serious than theoretical calculations of sampling error. They include refusals to be interviewed (non-response), question wording and question order, interviewer bias, weighting by demographic control data and screening (e.g., for likely voters). It is impossible to quantify the errors that may result from these factors."[7]

---

[7] Accessed August 10, 2005, http://www.harrisinteractive.com/harris ̇poll/index. asp?PID=579.

You might think that such an admission would undermine the value of such polling, but it remains a lucrative business and a principal tool for ascertaining and communicating public opinion. For our purposes, the concerns lie with the range of generalizations that might be made from them. Generalizations are, after all, inductive arguments that lend the conclusions a degree of probability but are always vulnerable to counterevidence. Are we prepared to accept the Harris poll's claims about adult Americans' opinions regarding troops in Iraq? Much may depend on the way the information is to be used. As it stands, the bias identified in the manner of selecting the sample points to a Fallacy of Biased Statistics in the reasoning behind the claims.

Pollsters try to prevent this kind of problem by using a sample that is randomly selected. This means that every member of the population has an equal probability of being selected. As we could see, the required access to a telephone meant that every American adult did not have an equal probability of being selected in the Harris poll. While randomness of this kind would eliminate a key potential bias, the preceding admission indicates other problems that could cause generalizations derived to be erroneous. While not errors of the status of fallacies, because they do not characterize regular patterns of incorrect argument, they are worth noting because of the way they can impact on generalized claims.

7 | Measurement Errors

Measurement Errors concern the reliability of the information collected (which may then be transformed into generalizations). Some problems can arise from what it is that is being measured. Political affiliation, for example, is something that is clearly understood by respondents, easily communicated, and easily translated into statistics. But questions that request an attitude or feeling from the respondents are more subjective. They may be misunderstood by those reviewing them and not easily communicated and then transferred into statistics.

Concerns of this nature were raised about a Web poll in October 2003, which is set out in the following case:

Case 8D

Politicians have approved the use of human embryos in some scientific research. Do you believe human embryos are human beings?

Yes . . . . 4,709 votes (30 percent)
No . . . . 11,022 votes (70 percent)

Total votes: 15,731

A respondent then complained that the wording allowed for significant abuse of the results:

> What answer can one give if . . . one does not believe human embryos are yet human beings, but disagrees on religious grounds with the use of human embryos in scientific research? A Negative response is likely to be interpreted as acceptance of embryonic research.

The concern is that the wording connects the issue of using human embryos in research with beliefs about the status of human embryos, *implying* that a respondent's attitude to the latter can be taken as an attitude to the former. Beyond this, though, is the much more controversial matter of what counts as a 'human being'. Belief about this is the property that the poll is supposedly measuring. But different people will have very different understandings of what counts as a human being. Arguably, this is what the poll is trying to ascertain, but there is a danger of compounding one vagueness with another. It is important, then, to ask how pollsters have arrived at the percentages they report.

The comments attached to the Harris poll alert us to other ways errors can arise with what is measured: people may not answer truthfully or may be unwilling to answer at all. Also, answers can be affected by the timing of a poll. For example, asking whether

U.S. troops should be withdrawn from Iraq just after a major loss of lives may elicit responses that are not truly reflective of the way people generally feel, but only of the way they feel for a short period.

The following constructed study captures a range of the concerns that we have seen connected to the generalizations of such studies and polls:

Case 8E

It would appear that having a busy social life wards off colds. In a recent study, common-cold viruses were sprayed into the noses of 276 healthy volunteers aged 18–55. Of those who had three or fewer roles or relationships, 62 percent got a cold. Of those with four or five kinds of social relationships, 43 percent got a cold. Of those with six or more kinds of relationships, 35 percent got a cold.

While this case deals with a study rather than a poll, the key concerns that have arisen in this section of the chapter are evident here, concerns that should lead us to find the generalization unreliable. The first problem lies with the sample of 276. This is typical of many studies, which, as Tversky and Kahneman have pointed out, are based on extremely small samples. It is hard to see how we can extrapolate from these 276 cases to the general population. Beyond this, how was the sample selected? It is not a random sample since the people involved are volunteers. And since volunteers self-select, we do not know whether this group is truly representative. A measurement problem with the generalization has to do with the key property of 'having a relationship'. How was this understood by the participants and by those who conducted the study? The reference to roles suggests that we are talking about relationships such as being a mother or brother. But having a number of roles or relationships does not mean one has a busy social life. The reasoning presented here, then, seems quite problematic with Fallacies of Insufficient Statistics and Biased Statistics present.

Critical Questions

A final set of Critical Questions will help us deal with the kinds of problems related to the sampling of polls and studies represented in Cases 8D and 8E.

1. Is the sample of sufficient size and representativeness to justify the generalizations made?
2. Is the property being measured free of problems of vagueness or misinterpretation that could affect the generalization?

Since a generalization is being made about a large group (the population) on the basis of only a sample of that group, we need first to ask how that sample was derived. Ideally, at least in polls, we want that sample to be random such that anyone in the population could be in the sample. This will increase the reliability of transferring conclusions from the sample to the population. In studies in which something specific (people who have a certain condition, for example) is being assessed, then general randomness is not desirable. But still the sample chosen must be duly representative of all people who have that condition. The sample must also be large enough to rule out chance or accidents. As we have seen, this size does not require a ratio of sample to population – samples of 1,000 are sufficient for nationwide polls – but cannot be unreasonably small.[8]

---

[8] Pollsters will try to address concerns with the sample by including a margin of error. Not much has been said about this here, although it was mentioned in the Harris poll discussed earlier in the chapter. A margin of error of ±3, for example, tells us that results may be inaccurate within that range (usually 95 times out of 100). Where responses created a significant result with 70 percent favoring one side and 30 percent the other, a margin of error of ±3 would not have an impact. But with closer results of, say, 48 percent against 52 percent, the same margin of error could mean an actual difference of 51 (48 + 3) against 49 (52 − 3), which changes the picture considerably.

Representativeness also requires that the sample be free from biases, and the first question covers this. We have seen several types of bias that could arise with a sample. The focus of this question should help us to detect any ways in which the sample is biased so as to favor a particular outcome.

The second question is concerned with the way a property believed to belong to the sample and population has been translated into statistics. Typically, properties that are more subjective in nature (what a sample 'feels' or 'believes') are more susceptible to errors, and we should worry how such feelings have been converted to statistics that are then broadly applied to a population. The vagueness of the concepts being measured may also affect the responses that are derived, further weakening the reliability of any generalizations.

Inductive arguments are so central to the everyday reasoning that we encounter and in which we engage that the fallacies associated with generalization may be some of the more prevalent. In this chapter, we have seen something of why this may be the case and how easy it can be to slip into errors of this kind. At the same time, a cautious review of such argumentation and careful questioning should help us to understand and avoid these problems.

CHAPTER EXERCISES

Assess the generalizations made or suggested in each of the following. Using the critical questions as a tool to justify your decisions, identify fallacies where they occur.

1. You are sure to enjoy Italy. We had wonderful weather for the two weeks we were there and we found the people so friendly.

2. We all have a duty to help others in need. My roommate definitely needs to write two papers tonight that are both due tomorrow. So, I should write one of them for her.

3. From a letter to the *Globe and Mail*, April 20, 2004, p. A16:

> Oakville, Ont. – For H. K. to state that Canadians believe seal hunting is acceptable is an incredible generalization. I am a Canadian, a vegan, and an animal activist. I certainly do not condone the savage act of seal hunting.
>
> My family and friends and all those I have encountered are also firmly opposed.
>
> There is no need to let all Canadians know how disgusted the British are, we feel the same way.

4. The following is an excerpted report of a study of university student behaviour undertaken by the University of Toronto and the City of Toronto Public Health Department ("Men use condoms more than women, study finds," *Toronto Star*, February 5, 1994, p. K11):

> A study of heterosexual students has found that men use condoms more often than women – and neither sex use them as often as they should. The survey of almost 500 students, undertaken by the University of Toronto and the City of Toronto Public Health Department, found 52 per cent of males regularly use condoms, compared with 40 per cent of females. Ted Myers, a professor with the university's department of health administration, says one factor might be that women are less assertive in demanding their partners use condoms. The study found that 10 per cent of women could not bring up the subject of condom use, compared with 3.5 per cent of men. "The fact that men are using condoms more frequently could be related to the fact they're having more sex partners," Myers adds. "Females are more likely to choose their partners and . . . do have fewer numbers of partners."

5. The following is a question and response from a Harris poll national sample of 1,000 U.S. adults, with a ±3 margin of error, "Origin of Human Life," conducted June 17–21, 2005, accessed August 20, 2005, http://www.pollingreport.com/science.htm#Stem:

Which of the following do you believe about how human beings came to be? Human beings evolved from earlier species. Human beings were created directly by God. Human beings are so complex that they required a powerful force or intelligent being to help create them.

Evolved from Earlier Species %	Created Directly By God %	Powerful Force/ Intelligent Being %	Unsure %
22	64	10	4

6. From a speech by the executive director of the Australia Institute to the Institute for Public Policy, reported in the *Independent*, March 11, 2004, accessed May 26, 2004, http://argument. independent.co.uk/podium/story.jsp?story=499944:

The pursuit of wealth and luxury is making us ill.

Last year, we asked Britons whether they could afford to buy everything they really need. Sixty per cent believe they can't. When we consider that Britain is one of the world's richest countries, and that Britons have real incomes nearly three times higher than in 1950, it is remarkable such a high proportion feel their incomes are inadequate. It is even more astonishing to note that when we separate the richest 20 per cent of the population, 46 per cent say they can't afford to buy everything they really need. In Australia and the USA, the proportion of the "suffering rich" is about the same.

...Despite the promises that maximising economic growth will give us a better society, we are in the grip of a plague of mental disorders and alienation. If we can discern no light to draw us on, no way out of our despondency, then what else do we do? Mental illness is a natural response to the hopelessness of modern consumer life.

7. A letter to the *LA Times*, May 29, 2004, accessed May 30, 2005, http://www.latimes.com/news/opinion/letters/la-le-reason29may 29,1,2228569.story?coll=la-news-comment-letters:

Widespread scientific illiteracy has left most Americans defenseless against pseudoscientific babble. The real problem is that many of these people vote. For fun, ask the next college-educated professional you meet to explain where liquid hydrogen, a proposed auto fuel, comes from and why it is not a "source" of energy. While most high school students in the 1950s could easily explain this, we have dumbed down our educational standards in math and science so far that public policy is now at risk. A population that believes in telepathy, fat-burning diet pills and a 10,000-year-old planet Earth is unable to evaluate anything objectively.

8. The following is from a CBS News poll that initially queried American adults on their views on evolution and creationism. Conducted during the Bush/Kerry presidential campaigns in November 2004, the poll then goes on to ask whether evolution and creationism should be taught in schools and identifies respondents according to whether they are Bush or Kerry supporters; accessed February 19, 2006, http://www.cbsnews.com/stories/2004/11/22/opinion/polls/main657083.shtml:

Overall, about two-thirds of Americans want creationism taught in school along with evolution. Only 37 percent want evolutionism replaced outright. More than half of Kerry voters want creationism taught alongside evolution. Bush voters are much more willing to want creationism to replace evolutionism altogether in a curriculum (just under half favor that), and 71 percent want it at least included.

FAVOR SCHOOLS TEACHING . . .

Creationism and evolution	
All Americans	65%
Kerry voters	56%
Bush voters	71%

Creationism instead of evolution	
All Americans	37%
Kerry voters	24%
Bush voters	45%

... This poll was conducted among a nationwide random sample of 885 adults interviewed by telephone November 18–21, 2004. There were 795 registered voters. The error due to sampling could be ±3 percentage points for results based on all adults and all registered voters.

9. Excerpted from a letter to the *Belfast Telegraph*, May 20, 2004, accessed May 22, 2004, http://www.belfasttelegraph.co.uk/news/letters/story.jsp?story=523132:

CONTRARY to the claims of the Belfast Telegraph's editorial (May 17), the Republic's smoking in public places ban must not come north. I am one of many people who cannot agree to such a move... The major argument in favour of this ban is the argument from passive smoking, which apparently kills hundreds of people each year. A ban on smoking in public places doesn't stop smokers from smoking, and, presumably, dying from the effects of smoking. So, this argument only has weight with regard to non-smokers.

But, why do non-smokers continually go to smoke-friendly pubs and restaurants? Apparently almost 80% of the population do not smoke. That's a massive amount of power, if only people were to accept responsibility for using it. If this 80% were to stop going to pubs and restaurants, telling the owners why they are abstaining, they would find that the policies of pubs and restaurants would change promptly. Instead, they continue to go and by so doing they consent to sitting in a smoky environment, as do the members of staff who work there. When you apply to work in a pub or a bar you know exactly the type of environment that is.

FURTHER READING

Amos Tversky and Daniel Kahneman's work on the devices humans use to draw conclusions from uncertain evidence, including generalizations, remains the best material for investigating the questions concerned (*Judgment under Uncertainty, Heuristics and Biases*, edited by D. Kahneman, P. Slovic, and A. Tversky

[Cambridge: Cambridge University Press, 1982]). For questions surrounding the conclusions drawn from polls, you should find help in Ralph Johnson, "Poll-ution: Coping with Surveys and Polls," in *Selected Issues in Logic and Communication*, edited by Trudy Govier (Belmont, CA.: Wadsworth, 1988), pp. 163–177.

CHAPTER 9

Correlation and Cause

1 Correlations and Causal Reasoning

Near the end of Chapter 8, Case 8E involved the drawing of a generalization from a study that tried to establish a correlation between two things – having a busy social life and avoiding colds. Implicit in the conclusion is the causal claim that the first thing, the busy social life, caused or was a causal factor in the occurrence of the second thing, avoiding colds. The Argument from Correlation to Cause can be a reasonable argumentation scheme if it meets the correct conditions,[1] but when these are not met, fallacious reasoning occurs.

In this chapter we will concentrate upon three types of causal reasoning that can prove problematic: (1) that which involves the concluding of a causal relation from a correlation or a mere temporal sequence, (2) reasoning that confuses the causal elements involved, and (3) that which predicts a negative causal outcome for a proposal or action, perhaps on the basis of an expected causal

---

[1] Douglas Walton, *Fundamentals of Critical Argumentation* (Cambridge: Cambridge University Press, 2006), pp. 100–101.

chain. The labels we will use for these three are *post hoc* reasoning, Misidentified Cause, and Slippery Slope reasoning.

Understanding causal reasoning and determining when it is fallacious are made difficult by the lack of any clear agreement on how to analyze the concept of causation. We will be able to detect cases in which something is clearly wrong with a causal argument, but more contentious cases will be a different matter. As Robert Pinto has pointed out,[2] *post hoc* reasoning need not be fallacious because showing some inference from a correlation to a cause can lend support to a causal hypothesis.

2 The *Post Hoc* Fallacy

The literature on fallacies provides two general interpretations of *post hoc* reasoning. The first of these will involve a causal inference on the basis of a temporal sequence and captures the full sense of the title of the argument: *post hoc ergo propter hoc* – after this, therefore because of this. The second type is the more difficult inference to a causal claim on the basis of a correlation. Since this is sometimes also presented under the title of the *post hoc*, we can treat both under this heading.

Accounts of the *post hoc* fallacy are traced to Aristotle's discussion of fallacies in his *Rhetoric* (Bk 2, Ch. 24, 1401b). There he writes:

Another line consists in representing as causes things which are not causes, on the ground that they happened along with or before the event in question. They assume that, because B happens after A, it happens because of A. Politicians are especially fond of this line. Thus Demades said that the policy of Demosthenes was the cause of all the mischief, "for after it the war occurred."

---

[2] Robert C. Pinto, "*Post Hoc Ergo Propter Hoc*," in *Fallacies: Classical and Contemporary Readings*, edited by Hans V. Hansen and Robert C. Pinto (University Park, PA: Penn State University Press, 1995), pp. 302–311.

Technically, Aristotle does not restrict the fallacy to cases in which there is temporal succession but allows that one event may have happened along with another.[3] But the point is that we connect two events causally when there is no justification for doing so, and perhaps the most obvious way in which people fall into this error occurs when one event precedes another, since we have learnt that effect follows cause in this way.

Case 9A

This case is from a report in the *LA Weekly* dealing with the circumstances surrounding a lunch between the film director Oliver Stone and the controversial French novelist Michel Houellebecq (June 24–30, 2005, http://www.laweekly.com/ink/05/31/features-bernhard.php):

You dine with Michel Houellebecq at your peril – just ask Oliver Stone. Shortly after sharing a table with the ultracontroversial French novelist at the White Lotus, a restaurant in Hollywood known for its deafening noise and nubile Asian clientele, the film director was pulled over by the cops on Sunset Boulevard and taken down to the station, charged with driving under the influence and possession of an illegal substance. It took a $15,000 bail to get him out. But then, nobody said hanging with the author of *The Elementary Particles* and *Platform* would be easy.

The reasoning that we can derive from this account is that dining with Houellebecq is a perilous activity and the evidence for this is that shortly after doing so, Stone was stopped by the police and charged with several offenses. The implicit assumption here

---

[3] As writers such as Charles Hamblin (*Fallacies* [London: Methuen, 1970], p. 79) have pointed out, while Aristotle includes a fallacy of treating a noncause as a cause in the *Sophistical Refutations* (167b), this is not a causal fallacy as the later textbooks have understood it. Aristotle is using the word 'cause' in a logical rather than scientific sense and refers to the same problem later in the *SR* as simply the insertion of irrelevant material.

is that since the charges followed lunch, it was the latter that was responsible. Arguably, Bernhard (the reporter) is not intending this to be a serious example, and the reasoning cannot be attributed to Stone himself.[4]

This does raise the question of how such a mistake would arise. It is clear that there is no obvious connection between the two events. Coincidence would account for things equally, if not more, easily. In fact, Pinto argues that if this fallacy is defined as reasoning in which someone concludes a causal connection on the basis of a temporal sequence of events, then he doubts it is possible for such reasoning to occur because it fails to meet a condition of minimal rationality (and so he would not call it 'reasoning' at all). Rather, Pinto points to the total context in which such reasoning occurs, including the individual's past experience. Such contexts include features of the background that would allow us implicitly to rule out other causal factors. For example, perhaps Stone *could have* attributed his arrest to his having lunched with Houellebecq if he understood that the police were keeping the foreign novelist under surveillance because of his notoriety. And if it had not been for that, no one would have noticed the amount that Stone drank at lunch immediately before driving away.

This does add some plausibility to the way such reasoning may occur. That other people are then fooled by it may be attributed to their own tendencies to reason in similar ways ("I lost my lucky rabbit foot and haven't been able to hit a home run since"). Or we can see Tversky and Kahneman's heuristics explanation come into play again: people focus on what is immediate and representative and do not invest in the kind of critical thinking needed to work through a situation. This observation turns what was an easily

---

[4] The further problem that you should see here is that the writer generalizes from the example to suggest that 'anyone' would find dining with the author perilous.

identifiable fallacy into a more difficult one, because once again we must try to review the context in which reasoning occurs in order to determine charitably whether a fallacy is committed. As we have with the Stone case, we will need to consider what plausible considerations a reasoner may have used in arriving at the causal claim. If no plausible contextual features are imaginable, or if the connection is still judged to be unwarranted, we may charge the fallacy.

The second variety of the *post hoc* fallacy is also difficult to judge. This involves the inference from a mere correlation to a causal claim. Unlike the one-off situations that characterize the previous type of examples, correlations involve a pattern of occurrences (often as the result of a study like those in Chapter 8). Since a criterion for establishing good causal claims is that they be supported by a clear correlation (Walton, p. 103), then what we are distinguishing here is unwarranted inferences from a correlation to a causal claim. The fact that two things occur together with regularity does not indicate that they are causally related. You can probably think of several examples of correlations that fit this description. Attendees at major supporting events tend to live within a certain geographical proximity to the venue where the event occurs, but living in the geographical area does not cause people to attend (nor vice versa). But information about such correlations is useful when owners and officials are deciding whether an area can support a major sports franchise.

Consider the following case:

Case 9B

It is not hard to see the impact of religion on society. In the 70s and 80s church attendance fell by as much as 30 percent. During that same period we saw an increase in common-law living, abortion, and inner-city crime, to name but a few. If we want to put society back on the rails we must return to our religious roots.

There are a number of assumptions made in this reasoning; the features that interest us are the feature that involves an inference from an alleged correlation between declining church attendance and declining social mores, and the assumption that the first causes the second. Thus, it is suggested, if we remedy the first (reverse the decline in church attendance by returning to our religious roots), we will change the second for the better. The problem here is that the causal link is not obvious, even once it is suggested, because coincidence could just as likely account for the occurrence of these two correlations at the same time. More work would have to be done to make the causal connection plausible; otherwise we have another instance of the *post hoc* fallacy.

The difficulty with such cases, though, is that this is a quite reasonable argument scheme. For example, when *Escherichia coli* (*E. coli*) increases in the water, people start to get sick. Here we have two correlations that are causally related. So we need some criterion to help us decide whether a causal claim is legitimate or not. Again, we are taken to the context of the reasoning for this. Experience has helped to confirm the *E. coli*–sickness relationship, first to suggest it as a hypothesis, and then to confirm that hypothesis through testing. Where such background does not exist (or does not seem plausible) we have cause for concern. At the same time, of course, arguments of this type are often intended to *establish* the causal link where it was not understood, that is, to suggest the hypothesis to be tested. In such cases, we are restricted to what is plausible on the basis of other experience. We are looking here to rule out coincidence. The onus really lies with the person making the inference from a correlation to a causal relationship. But in the absence of someone who meets that obligation, you can still argue for the greater likelihood of coincidence in any particular case. With respect to Case 9B, for example, societies change in all kinds of ways over time, and there are bound to be correlations between changes that occur at the same time without any causal connection between them (consider how the average incomes increased in Western countries during the period when pop music became popular). Without a specific reason to see two things as causally related, an arguer is engaging in fallacious reasoning.

3 | Misidentifying the Cause

The *post hoc* fallacy involves attributing a causal relationship where none exists. Other problems related to causal reasoning involve mistakes about an actual causal link. Two such errors involve types of misidentification of causes. In the first instance, we may falsely identify X as the cause of Y when on closer inspection a third factor, Z, is the cause of both X and Y. In the second case, we may confuse a cause and effect: identifying X as the cause of Y, when it is actually Y that causes X.

The first of these, overlooking the real causal factor behind events, points to the difficulty of working with causal reasoning and identifying when it has gone wrong. What was the *cause* of the flooding of New Orleans in August 2005? The hurricane, Katrina? Building a city below sea level? Inadequate levees to hold back flood waters? Earlier political decisions not to invest money in strengthening the levees? A full analysis would likely allow that all or most of these prior events were causal factors in the resulting disaster. In fact, we recognize that most causes are complex and we can rarely identify one thing that counts as *the* cause.[5] So it is not surprising that people will sometimes not look at the full picture and so fail to see a causal agent acting behind others.

---

[5] What analysts will often try to do is identify a necessary cause, that is, one that, if taken away, would prevent the effect from occurring. These are distinguished from sufficient causes, which can result in an effect, but in the absence of which that effect could still occur if another sufficient cause were active.

Case 9C

The decision of large numbers of women in the last decades of the twentieth century to abandon the home and instead pursue careers in the workplace has led to a decrease in the birthrate, since fewer are making the decision to stay home and be mothers.

There is something a little circular about the reasoning here, but our interest is in whether this expresses a plausible causal relationship. Presumably, we could find correlations in studies that show that birthrates decreased during the same period that more women chose careers over homes. But if we look behind these two factors, we see that things like advances in medical technology, specifically in contraception, have made possible both effects. It is not so much that choosing a career over motherhood has caused a decline in the birthrate, but that widely available access to contraception has allowed women both to enter the work force in greater numbers and to plan their families better. In all cases in which causal relationships are suggested, we should look beyond them to the wider context in which they arise to see whether there could plausibly be a common cause that can account for both factors. Otherwise, we risk committing or being deceived by a fallacy of Misidentified Cause.

The second type of misidentifying a cause may be a little easier to detect if we are alert to its possible presence. To argue, for example, that the presence of a women's shelter has led to an increase in crimes against women because the statistics show more reported assaults after the shelter is established than before (that is, the correlation is there) misses the causal relationship. It is the sexual assaults that create the need for, and thereby cause, the existence of the shelter, and once women have a safe venue to report to, there is an increase of *reported* assaults. Thus, it is not that X (the women's shelter) causes Y (the increase in assaults), but that Y (the assaults) causes X (the shelter).

The following case captures how crucial this mistake can be:

Case 9D

Antony Beevor notes that after the defeat of Germany, German officers and civilians tried to persuade their conquerors, the United States and Britain, to ally themselves with Germany against the Soviets.[6] Beevor writes:

The fact that it was Nazi Germany's onslaught against the Soviet Union in 1941 which had brought Communism to all of central and southeast Europe – something which all the revolutions between 1917 and 1921 had failed to do – remained beyond their understanding... the Nazis had seized upon their own country's fatal tendency to confuse cause and effect.

As Beevor understands the reasoning of many Germans at the time, Nazi Germany's war with the Soviet Union was the effect (caused by) Communist expansion into central and southeast Europe, whereas in fact the causal relationship had been the other way around. What such people identified as the effect (Nazi Germany's attack on the Soviet Union) was the cause, and the Communist expansion was the effect. Such a widespread misapprehension, as Beevor reports it, was the result of state propaganda, something to which many people are susceptible. Thus, in this case the fallacious reasoning can be explained by a deception. But in other cases, a Hasty Conclusion may result in a failure to think through the likely causal relations involved and thus reverse them by mistake. Again, the fallacy involved would be that of a Misidentified Cause.

The three types of causal fallacies we have discussed so far can be identified and evaluated if we employ certain Critical

---

[6] Antony Beevor, *The Fall of Berlin 1945* (New York: Viking, 2002), p. 430.

Questions that focus on the relationships involved and any underlying correlations.

Critical Questions

1. Is there a correlation supporting the causal claim? That is,
   are there a number of cases on which the claim is grounded?
2. Can the move from the correlation to the alleged causal link
   be explained by coincidence?
3. Is the causal claim itself credible? That is, are the cause and
   effect correctly identified and has an underlying common
   cause of both clearly been ruled out?

The first question explores the grounds for the causal claim. Is it
one based on an alleged correlation between two variables, so that
they appear to increase or decrease together, or one increases while
the other decreases? Some causal claims are not supported by such
reasoning, so it is important to look first for an actual correlation
study, an anecdotal correlation suggestion, or no suggested correlation at all. These decrease in weakness of support. The absence
of a correlation does not mean that two things are not causally
related. But it does put the onus on the arguer to show why we
should believe they are. And in particular, we need to accept that
the relationship could not be no more than coincidence.

The second question takes the concern over coincidence further
and asks whether the relationship shown by the correlation could
be just coincidence. This requires us to draw on the contextual
factors that support the inference from a correlation to a causal
link. In the absence of such a plausible inference, we may expect
the *post hoc* fallacy to be present.

Once we are sure we have a causal link, grounded in some evidence, we need also to be sure that the expressed causal relationship is correct. The third question directs us to ask whether it

may be that B causes A, rather than that A causes B, and whether there may be a hidden common cause that is responsible for both A and B. Again, this will require a fuller examination of whatever contextual features are available, or, in the absence of those, an assessment of the plausibility given what we know generally about the situation. It is such an assessment that allows us to look at the antecedent events that preceded the entry of greater numbers of women into the work force in the seventies and identify the wide access to the new technology of the birth-control pill as a plausible causal factor for that, along with a declining birthrate. Of course, other factors could also be involved; that is why the reasoning involved is open to objection and defeat. Our job in our evaluations is to provide the best explanations we can.

4 The Argument from Consequences

The Argument from Consequences is a scheme that can have positive and negative variants (Walton, pp. 104–106). As an argument that draws on causal reasoning, it projects a consequence that will likely follow as a result of some action or policy. Depending on whether the consequence is deemed positive or negative, the action or policy is recommended or rejected. In such arguments the crucial factors to consider are the likelihood that the consequences will be caused by what is proposed and the reasons that have been given for believing so.

Consider the following case:

Case 9E
One proposal that often concerns postsecondary education students and their parents is that tuition should be introduced where it does not exist or increased where it does in order to produce or maintain high-quality education. The following is an extract from

a response to such a proposal (*Globe and Mail*, September 8, 2005, A14):

[P]aying more for [education] will not guarantee "excellence" and will not provide students with a better return on their "investment." It will, however, ensure that university students and their parents experience a lifelong engagement with crushing student loans, outstanding lines of credit, mortgage debt and collection agencies.

This argument to negative consequences is a rebuttal of an argument to positive consequences (more tuition equals a better education) made in the editorial the previous day. The reasoning here is that tuition should not be increased in part because doing so will cause serious financial burdens for students and their parents. In considering whether this reasoning is fallacious we need to weigh the likelihood that the predicted consequence will follow. That likelihood is decreased by the generalization made – the consequence is predicted to befall students and their parents generally. But, while *some* people are plausibly affected in this way, there are all sorts of reasons related to parental incomes, education saving plans, and future employment incomes that undermine the claim. It is simply too strong. Moreover, no specific reasons have been given for believing that these consequences, rather than others, will follow. Nor has the arguer given evidence against the previous argument to positive consequences other than a matching claim of negative consequences. In sum, the argument commits a fallacy of Argument from Consequences.

This evaluation matches the critical questions provided by Walton (p. 106) for this argument scheme. Briefly, we have asked first how likely it is that the consequence will follow; second, what evidence is provided for believing the consequence will follow; and third, whether there are consequences of the opposite value that should be considered. The argument in Case 9E does not fare well against any of these questions.

5 │ The Fallacy of the Slippery Slope

The final fallacy that we will consider in this chapter is the frequently committed Slippery Slope. In fact, this is one fallacy that is so widely found that the term is likely to be more familiar to you than the names of other fallacies we have explored. But as scholarship in the last few decades has shown, Slippery Slope reasoning itself is not inherently fallacious, as earlier textbooks claimed. Again, that claim was due in part to a failure to explore real cases fully and consider what was at stake.

Slippery Slope reasoning is a type of negative reasoning from consequences, distinguished by the presence of a causal chain leading from the proposed action to the negative outcome. In its most straightforward form, the argument includes a crucial premise in which it is maintained that the proposed action will (or probably will) lead to a series of causally connected actions.[7]

Case 9F

The debates in several Western nations over the merits of same-sex marriage (and the subsequent enabling legislation in some) have led to a range of arguments opposing such an idea on the basis of the likely consequences. The following is a brief extract from one such discussion, accessed May 23, 2004, http://www.family.org/cforum/extras/a0032427.cfm:

First, when the State sanctions homosexual relationships and gives them its blessing, the younger generation becomes confused about sexual identity and quickly loses its understanding of lifelong commitments, emotional bonding, sexual purity, the role of children in a family, and from a spiritual perspective, the "sanctity" of marriage.

---

[7] Variants of this can include a premise in which only one causal step is given between the proposed action and the consequence (unlike the argument from negative consequence, which goes straight from the action to the consequence with no intervening step) or a set of simultaneous events rather than a series.

Marriage is reduced to something of a partnership that provides attractive benefits and sexual convenience, but cannot offer the intimacy described in Genesis. Cohabitation and short-term relationships are the inevitable result. Ask the Norwegians, the Swedes, and the people from the Netherlands. That is exactly what is happening there.

As in many Slippery Slope arguments, the conclusion in this one is implicit: we do not want the final consequence in the series (cohabitation and short-term relationships) to occur and so we should not take the first step, which is to allow the state to sanction same-sex relationships/marriages. The core premise in the argument is the causal premise, which presents two links. As a first causal step, the younger generation will become "confused about sexual identity" and lose its understanding of a range of things related to relationships. This in turn will lead (inevitably) to the second step of cohabitation and short-term relationships.

Good Slippery Slope arguments will present causal links that are plausible (while not guaranteed) and a consequence that is clearly negative. The argument in Case 9F, by contrast, does neither. We have no obvious reason to think that legislation to permit one segment of society to marry will cause a whole generation to become confused about their sexual identity (for some, it could have the opposite effect). Nor would we expect that generation "quickly" to lose its understanding of life-long relationships. If anything, it would witness an expanded range of such examples. The next step to cohabitation and short-term relationships is also not obvious. While an increase in cohabitation might well occur in coming decades, the factors influencing that may already be in place, since we currently see such a trend in some societies, so linking this to state sanctioning of homosexual relationships requires considerable argumentation that is not present. In effect, the arguer is implying that the proposal would lead to the end of traditional marriage even in heterosexual communities, and that is a jump unwarranted by anything provided here.

Finally, the negative factor concerns the undesirability of the consequence. Arguably, the immediate audience for this argument would find widespread cohabitation and short-term relationships, rather than traditional marriages, undesirable. But the larger audience that would be affected by such a change in social policy may not see this as undesirable. In sum, we have grounds for judging this argument to be fallacious, and the fallacy in question is that of the Slippery Slope.

Critical Questions

The discussion of Case 9F indicates the kinds of Critical Questions we need to employ in identifying and assessing potentially fallacious Slippery Slopes. We can express such questions as follows:

1. Is each of the causal steps plausible?
2. Could one stop and go back, or is the "slope" clearly slippery?
3. Is the alleged outcome really negative?

The first question both captures the identifying feature of this type of argument to a negative consequence and serves as the core evaluative question. Of the forward-looking causal steps, whether single or plural, simultaneous or sequential, we must inquire about the likelihood that they will occur as a result of the proposed action. In assessing this, we will be drawing on previous Critical Questions that we used for general causal reasoning. If any step fails to be plausible, or is clearly unlikely to occur, then we can assign the fallacy label to the argument in question. It also matters how strongly the causal claims are made. The argument in Case 9F included the claim that the second causal link would be "inevitable." As we have appreciated, such claims require far more evidence than weaker claims about what is "likely" to follow. Arguments involving such claims are also clearly susceptible to counterinstances.

Slippery Slope arguments are characteristically just that – slopes. The assumption is that once we start down this causal slope we slide on toward the consequence. So it is important to ask, as the second question invites us to do, whether the causal argument being proposed is unstoppable or irreversible. This may be another way to question the plausibility of any causal link in the argument, because if we can stop on the slope, then the next point need not arrive. But the sense of something's being irreversible is also implicit in many of these arguments, and sometimes critics may judge that the effects of a proposal could simply be reversed or positively altered.

The latter point leads us to the third critical question, which asks how really negative the conclusion is. This consideration is often overlooked, but it is an important feature of the reasoning involved. The possibility of reversing the outcome if it led to bad consequences is one reason not to find them to be so negative. If, on balance, the proposal offers a lot if it works and could be reversed if it does not, then there is every reason to go through with it. It may also happen that what an arguer considers to be a negative consequence would simply not be judged that way by a wider audience. Some dog owners believe that legislation restricting certain "aggressive" breeds would lead to an underground trade in such animals. But the general population, alarmed by frequent dog attacks, might not view that consequence so negatively.

6 Distinguishing Causal Slopes from Precedents

A final point to note about Slippery Slope arguments looks ahead to one of the strategies of the next chapter. Sometimes an argument is made against a proposal because it will lead to the occurrence of other cases like it – it will set a precedent. Here, the reasoning is essentially analogical and is based on an underlying principle of fairness that we treat similar cases similarly. By contrast, Slippery Slope reasoning as we have discussed it here is essentially *causal* in nature. It tells us that one event will likely *cause* another. Reasoning based on Precedent tells us that something will follow because it is *like* what is being proposed. These two types of reasoning are easy to confuse, and some arguments will even employ both strategies. But it will be important for you to distinguish between them because what makes for fallacious cases of each kind is very different.

CHAPTER EXERCISES

Using the Critical Questions and considerations of this chapter, assess the following:

1. We should not teach sex education in high schools because teaching it causes sexual experimentation that would not occur otherwise.

2. The following example concerns the U.S. Fox News cable show:

   I am concerned about the degree of disinformation that Fox dispenses to its audiences on a daily basis. Certainly, as America's most popular cable news network, it deserves some of the blame for the fact that more than one-third of Americans still believe Saddam Hussein was responsible for the 9/11 attacks.

3. The following is a letter to the *Independent*, July 22, 2004, accessed July 24, 2004, http://argument.independent.co.uk/letters/story.jsp?story=543710:

   Sir: I suppose the Government will try to claim responsibility for falling crime. However, we know that the real credit should go to the 1960s, when a new attitude of love, peace and understanding was born.

4. A television advertisement for Smarties shows two men in an office having the following dialogue. You will need to extract the reasoning of the second man.

First man in office: I thought you were supposed to eat the red ones last?

Second man in office: Yeah. The Smarties people have been saying that for years. But yesterday I ate the red ones first.

First man: And?

Second man: You know Vanessa from Finance?

First man: Yeah.

Second man: Well, this morning she walked by my office.

First man: And?

Second man: She never walks by my office.

Both men: Hello!

5. Canada's Supreme Court had just ruled on a case so as to allow private health care in Canada. The head of the Council of Canadians contributed a letter to the *Globe and Mail*, June 11, 2005, from which the following is excerpted:

In their decision, the Supreme Court justices used the example of the United Kingdom, Germany and Switzerland to show that private insurance can coexist with a public system. Many commentators who support two-tiered health care jumped on these examples as the kind of kinder, gentler privatization they have in mind, saying they do not want the U.S. model.

These proponents of a two-tier system would do well to remember that we do not have a free-trade agreement with these European countries. We do, however, have NAFTA, in which rules are very clear. The exemption for health care, which has largely kept the big U.S. for-profit health corporations out of Canada, applies only to a fully publicly funded system delivered on a non-commercial basis. Once privatized, the system must give "national treatment" rights to U.S. private hospital chains and HMOs, which cannot be treated differently than Canadian for-profit companies. Not only would U.S. health corporations have the right to set up shop in Canada, they would have the same right to public funding as Canadian companies. In no time, the public system would be bankrupt and we would have an Americanized corporate health-care system.

6. Examples in the Chapter Exercises in Chapter 6 referred to the controversial article "The Kindness of the Hunt," published in newspapers across the world, in which the British novelist Frederick Forsyth defended the tradition of foxhunting in Britain and argued for its continuance on the grounds that the culling of foxes is necessary and the fox hunt is the kindest (most efficient and humane) way to go about it. The following extract is from that article.

The end of the hunt would force farmers to turn to the gun, farmers are not marksmen (the fox is "a blur in the undergrowth"), so most foxes would be maimed and left to die in agony.

7. The following is an excerpt from a report titled "Abortion and Crime," *National Post*, August 17, 1999, p. A18, that describes the research done by Levitt and Donohue:

Mr. Levitt and Mr. Donohue argue that those people most likely to end up committing crimes – the "unwanted" children of poor, unwed, teenage mothers from "minority" communities – were aborted in disproportionately high numbers in the early 1970s. Now, in the 1990s, when these children would have entered the age group with the highest rate of criminal activity, we find crime rates are actually down.

8. In summer 1935, a new company emerged with a new product. The company was Penguin and the product was paperback books. Paperbacks were seen as a response to the need for good-quality contemporary fiction at a cheap price. But they had their critics. The following is from a letter by the novelist George Orwell to *New English Weekly*, March 5, 1936:

In my capacity as a reader I applaud the Penguin Books; in my capacity as a writer I pronounce them anathema. Hutchinsons are now bringing out a very similar edition, though only of their own books, and if other publishers follow suit, the result may be a flood of cheap reprints which will cripple the lending libraries and check the output of new novels. This would be a fine thing for literature, but it would be a very bad thing for trade, and when you have to choose between art and money – well, finish it for yourself.

9. The following is excerpted from a longer piece opposing dance as a legitimate activity in which humans should engage. Accessed May 20, 2005, http://www.bible.ca/s-dancing.htm, it is intended for a primarily Christian audience:

Who can deny that the body contact between the sexes and the bodily movements associated with dances to modern rock music lead to sexual arousal? In fact, some advocates of dancing stress such to be an outlet for sexual urges. The whole range of the modern dance is designed to express or convey a message, namely, "love-making" and is calculated to be sexually stimulating.

It is understood, of course, that the sex urge is God-given and is not sinful per se. Yet, God-given desires must have God-appointed boundaries; the righteous fulfillment of the sex urge is limited to the marriage relationship (I Corinthians 7:1–9). To engage in any activity which produces lewd emotions or excites unlawful sexual desire is "lasciviousness" and stands condemned by God (Galatians 5:19–21). Let none be deceived; the basic appeal of the modern dance, as admitted even by its proponents, has its foundation in human passion. Obviously, not every person who engages in dancing ends up a prostitute or fornicator, yet many who have come to immoral ends began their journey by way of the dance.

Let none be deceived, the fruit of the modern dance has never increased purity and spirituality, but the destruction of all that relates to human happiness and eternal salvation.

10. The following is a letter to *The Australian*, July 26, 2004, accessed July 27, 2004, http://www.theaustralian.news.com.au/storypane/ 0,9421,4^8^21682,00.html, Mark Latham, MP, is a member of the Australian Labour Party:

Kevin Rugg (Letters, 26/7) suggests that Mark Latham's youthful puff of the stuff has had long-term psychiatric impacts. Mr Latham mightn't be the only such casualty.

When one runs through the names of Australia's most prominent right-wing commentators and intellectuals, one is struck by the large proportion who were involved with the academic Left and/or the student Left in their youth from the 1950s through to the '80s. In many cases this included involvement in anarchist or revolutionary Marxist groups, or in the more avant-garde elements of the new social movements.

The recreational substances imbibed in those circles would have been a good deal harder than anything Mr Latham inhaled. There is, therefore, ample scope for an interdisciplinary research project on the linkages between the illicit drug usage of our conservative commentariat during their radical youth, the long-term impacts on their brains, and their drift to the Right later in life.

FURTHER READING

Robert Pinto's essay on the *post hoc, Fallacies: Classical and Contemporary Readings*, edited by Hans V. Hansen and Robter C. Pinto [University Park, PA: Penn State University Press, 1995], pp. 302–311), is an excellent place to begin exploring the complexities of this kind of reasoning. Two good sources for further reading on Slippery Slope arguments are Trudy Govier, "What's Wrong with Slippery Slope Arguments?" in *The Philosophy of Argument* (Newport News, VA: Vale Press, 1999), pp. 69–82, and Douglas Walton, *Slippery Slope Arguments* (Oxford: Clarendon Press, 1992).

CHAPTER 10

Analogical Reasoning

1 Principles of Analogy

One clear strategy of argumentation when reasoning about things that are uncertain is to see whether they are similar to things that we do know and then draw conclusions about them on the basis of the similarities. Logicians call this strategy the 'Argument from Analogy'. An analogy is a comparison of two things or analogues. For example, Julian Huxley offered the following comparison: "The relation between predator and prey in evolution is somewhat like that between methods of attack and defence in the evolution of war."[1] In comparing these two things, Huxley hopes to shed light on the first pair because of what we know about the second pair. But Huxley is not here providing an Argument from Analogy, and the first thing we should note is not to assume that the presence of an analogy in argumentation means the argument scheme is being used. Huxley provides no details of how the two pairs are alike; nor, crucially, does he draw a conclusion on the basis of the

[1] Julian Huxley, *Evolution: The Modern Synthesis* (London: Allen & Unwin, 1942), p. 495.

similarities. This latter feature is a key identifying feature of the Argument from Analogy.

The basic fallacy associated with the Argument from Analogy is called False Analogy. Understanding how the scheme works[2] does not explain how false analogies can arise and what it is that is wrong with them, but it does help us appreciate how analogical reasoning differs from the other types of reasoning we have discussed.[3]

While the Argument from Analogy has a long history of use in philosophical texts, stretching back to at least the *Dialogues* of Plato, Hamblin attributes the earliest mention of the fallacy False Analogy to the Elizabethan writer Abraham Fraunce, who treats it as part of a secondary list of fallacies.[4] Hamblin himself has little to say about this particular fallacy. Modern treatments of False Analogy can be quite varied in their remarks and often disagree as to exactly what is at stake when the correct argument scheme goes wrong. Van Eemeren and Grootendorst suggest the problem lies in a defective comparison such that it is not really justified because there are crucial differences between the two things being compared.[5] Trudy Govier, in one of her treatments of the Argument from Analogy,[6] raises the concern about analogies that are loose and far-fetched. The appeal in such arguments is to highly superficial similarities that give no real support to the conclusion. The possibility of these two distinct problems should help us to

---

[2] For the explanation of this see Douglas Walton, *Fundamentals of Critical Argumentation* (Cambridge: Cambridge University Press, 2006), pp. 96–99.

[3] As you work through this chapter, you will realize that some of the generalization arguments in Chapter 8 are based on analogies between past and present experience and between samples and populations.

[4] Charles L. Hamblin, *Fallacies* (London: Methuen, 1970), p. 142.

[5] Frans van Eemeren and Rob Grootendorst, *Argumentation, Communication, and Fallacies: A Pragma-Dialectical Perspective* (Mahwah, NJ: Erlbaum, 1992), p. 163.

[6] Trudy Govier, *A Practical Study of Argument*, 6th ed. (Belmont, CA: Wadsworth, 2005), p. 379.

appreciate what can go wrong with arguments based in analogical reasoning.

2 | False Analogy

Govier's theoretical work on arguments from analogy draws from some earlier unpublished lectures of the philosopher John Wisdom in identifying two types of analogical arguments – those that are inductive in nature and others that are hypothetical and are called a priori analogies.[7] This is an important distinction to observe because the analogical arguments you find will fall into one of these categories.

Inductive analogies fit the definition that was provided earlier for basic analogical arguments. In such arguments, a prediction is made about a case by comparing it with an actual known case. By contrast, what Govier calls a priori analogies (Wisdom called them case-by-case reasoning) do not draw from real examples but tend to be based on thought experiments; that characteristic is what makes them hypothetical or a priori (which means "prior to experience"). Rather than predictions, a priori analogies issue in proposals for action. A famous example of this that you may have encountered is Judith Thomson's analogy between a woman who is carrying an unwanted fetus and someone involuntarily hooked up to a dying violinist. This case is clearly hypothetical, but its power lies in the types of similarities that we might accept between the two cases and the conclusion we might draw about the legitimacy of abortion on the basis of those similarities. The first two cases in this chapter will further illustrate this distinction.

---

[7] See Govier's discussions of this distinction in her *Problems in Argument Analysis and Evaluation* (Dordrecht: Foris, 1987), Chapter 4, and *The Philosophy of Argument* (Newport News, VA: Vale Press,1999), Chapter 9.

Case 10A

The following is a letter to *The Guardian*, July 11, 2004, accessed July 20, 2004, http://www.guardian.co.uk/letters/story/ 0,3604,1258079,00.html:

The refusal to face up to the consequences of climate change is analogous to the church's historical acceptance of slavery. Indeed, fossil fuels and slavery are both sources of power. Until we accept that the destruction wrought by the use of fossil fuels is morally unacceptable, we shall not find the passion to force societies to change. We all need to make our leaders wake up, just as Wilberforce did. But it took him 30-odd years and we do not have that luxury.

There is no mistaking this as an Argument from Analogy; the author flags the fact for us by claiming the cases of refusing to accept the consequences of climate change (the primary analogue) and the historical acceptance of slavery (the comparator analogue) are analogous. And this is an inductive analogy – it deals in real rather than hypothetical cases and issues in a prediction that the primary analogue is morally unacceptable. This conclusion is indeed contentious, but it gains its alleged inductive strength from a stated similarity between the two (they are both sources of power) and unstated similarities the audience might provide, and our agreement that the main property of moral unacceptability describes the comparator analogue.

Yet we may have real misgivings about the argument here. One of the warnings earlier was to be wary of Arguments from Analogy in which the similarities are superficial and give no real support to the conclusion. There may be a subtle shift in the meaning of 'power' as it describes fossil fuels and slavery, but of more concern is that this may be an incidental similarity (if it is one) rather than an essential one. To decide this, we look to the overall conclusion that the destruction wrought by fossil fuels is *morally* unacceptable. That fossil fuels are a source of power, while acceptable, does not seem to bear on the morality of their use. In fact, this is what needs to be addressed in this argument. Why should we think the destruction wrought by fossil fuels is like the oppression of human beings who had their decision-making power taken away from them and were forced to live in servitude, often under inhuman conditions? In this sense, the two analogues do not seem obviously similar. Note how much this argument scheme requires us both to delve into the context and to use our imaginations. The fallaciousness of the reasoning may not appear readily before us; we need instead to draw it out. False Analogy is more complex in its demands on us than other fallacies have been.

Failing to be persuaded that there is sufficient similarity between two cases is not the same as determining that there are relevant dissimilarities between the two cases. That was the other principal concern that was noted earlier: the comparison is defective because there are crucial differences. As we noted in Chapter 2, relevance is a relationship, and so we should ask here to what the differences should be relevant. The answer is the main property of moral unacceptability (the same property to which the similarities were compared). Slavery involved the mistreatment of autonomous human beings and violated their rights. The destruction from fossil fuels does not obviously do anything like this. The use of fossil fuels is something about which we have an open debate such that those affected are prepared to live with the costs because they give higher value to the benefits. That slavery is now seen to be at odds with all major moral systems (such as Kantianism and utilitarianism) supports its immorality; the same is not the case with the use of fossil fuels.

On balance, then, when we explore what goes wrong in Case 10A we find the argument weakened by insufficient relevant similarities and relevant dissimilarities, which render it an example of False Analogy.

Case 10B

After a gunman killed a number of children in a school in Scotland in March 1996, the British government introduced legislation to control the use of guns, including those employed in sports. Commenting on the legislation, a member of the British royal family offered the following argument to BBC radio (reported in the *Globe and Mail*, December 20, 1996):

If a cricketer, for instance, suddenly decided to go into a school and batter a lot of people to death with a cricket bat, which he could do very easily, I mean are you going to ban cricket bats? There's no evidence that people who use weapons for sport are any more dangerous than people who use golf clubs or tennis racquets or cricket bats. Guns are no more dangerous than cricket bats and should not be banned.

In contrast to Case 10A, the analogy employed here is a priori. It is based on the hypothetical, rather than real, case of supposing that a cricketer enters a school and uses his bat as a weapon. Since guns are no more dangerous than cricket bats, and since we would not ban cricket bats in the hypothetical case, then guns should not be banned. The issue here is not really whether the two cases are similar, as it was for inductive analogies, but whether the comparator analogue (cricket bats used as weapons)[8] "has features which show the correctness of a certain decision with regard to the primary case" (Govier, 1999, p. 139).

Yet, again, the argument should strike us as more than just fanciful; there is something wrong with it that makes it quite unpersuasive. The major concern here is the striking dissimilarities between the analogues, which are directly relevant to the conclusion. While the point is often made that it is people that kill, not

---

[8] In fact, this argument has several comparator analogues, since golf clubs and tennis racquets are also mentioned. For our purposes, it is sufficient to restrict the discussion to cricket bats.

guns, it remains the case that guns are a traditional instrument of killing and cricket bats are not; it is far easier to kill with a gun than a bat; and statistically, when a weapon is sought a gun will be favoured over a bat. Perhaps restricting the availability of guns will compel people to choose other forms of weapons, such as cricket bats, but that is not relevant to this argument and would have to be addressed separately should it occur. So the hypothetical case offered here does not open things up and introduce a useful comparator that sheds insight on the matter. Rather, it diverts the dialogue in a confused direction. A False Analogy results.

Critical Questions

The discussion of these two cases points to several Critical Questions that will help you to identify and evaluate False Analogies.

1. Is the argument in question one that clearly uses an Argument from Analogy, and is the analogy used inductive or a priori in nature?
2. In the case of inductive analogies used in an argument, are the similarities provided or suggested incidental or essential to the conclusion being made (the main property being predicted of the primary analogue)?
3. In the case of inductive and a priori analogies used in an argument, are there dissimilarities between the analogues that undermine the claim in the conclusion?

The rationale and value of these questions should be clear from what has preceded. In the first instance, we must be certain that an Argument from Analogy is being used, rather than just a comparison of some nature inserted into a piece of reasoning with no conclusion drawn from the comparison. It is the Argument *from* Analogy that is in question here. Once we are satisfied that we have correctly identified the scheme, we must decide whether the analogy is inductive, using real cases and issuing in a prediction, or a priori, using a hypothetical case and issuing in a recommendation or proposed action.

The real cases of inductive analogies can then be scrutinized for the quality of their similarities. These should be essential to the analogy in that they bear on the main property predicted of the primary analogue in the conclusion. Some arguers will avoid part of their burden of proof and expect us to imagine the similarities between cases (probably because they feel them to be obvious). This will be difficult or easier, depending on our experience. Treat this as an invitation from the arguer to be drawn into the argument and contribute to its development. This is what is likely to happen in the exchanges of a dialogue anyway. Where the comparison is implausible, too loose, or based only on incidental features of similarity, you have grounds for charging the argument to be a False Analogy.

Finally, both types of analogy should not have relevant dissimilarities that undermine the conclusion. When this happens, you will be able to support a charge of False Analogy. But, again, this will require some imaginative probing. List ways in which the analogues are different from each other, and then decide whether any of these differences is enough to make a real difference to the conclusion.

3 | Fallacious Appeal to Precedent

There are other fallacies that are analogical in nature. In the last chapter, we explored Slippery Slope reasoning as a possible causal fallacy. It was noted that the Slippery Slope bore resemblance to another argument scheme that was based on analogical rather than causal reasoning. This is the Appeal to Precedent. Underlying this argument is the principle of fairness, which exhorts us to treat similar cases similarly. If a particular action is performed, so the reasoning goes, it will commit us to treating other cases in the same way in the future. But we have reasons for not wanting to be so obligated (the consequences are undesirable), and so we should not perform the initial action.

You can see that this argument will have a structure very similar to that of the Slippery Slope, and, hence, there will be a tendency to confuse the two. But the reasoning underlying the Slippery Slope tells us that one action will (or may) *cause* another, and so on; whereas the reasoning under the Appeal to Precedent tells us a consequence will follow because one action or case is *like* (analogous to) another. The difference is crucial if we want to evaluate arguments of each type competently.

A variant of the Appeal to Precedent is an argument that tells us a precedent exists, and therefore, on grounds of consistency, we are committed to treating other cases in the same way and must act, legislate, or proceed accordingly. In both types of Appeal to Precedent the key determinant in whether the reasoning is strong or fallacious is whether the cases really are analogous as claimed or implied.

Case 10C

The following is a letter to the *Globe and Mail*, Thursday, June 19, 2003 p. A16. Prior to the sanctioning of same-sex marriages in Canada in summer 2005, there was a serious weighing of the pros and cons of such a move. This argument contributed to that debate.

The liberal government plans to endorse same-sex marriage based on a lower-court ruling in Ontario (Ottawa Backs Gay Marriage – June 18). Once it does, the well-defined definition of traditional marriage in Canada will be forever altered. If we allow people to marry without regard to their sex, who is to say that we can't discriminate on the basis of number? It is a small step then to legalizing polygamy. Once we open up marriage beyond the boundary of one man and one woman only, there will be no difference based on the Charter of Rights and Freedoms between gay marriage and polygamous marriage. Do we want to erode our societal values based on the whims of a small minority? I hope not, and let's not abuse the Charter in this way.

You should recognize this as a case we reviewed in a preliminary way when we were starting to consider the nature of fallacious arguments (Case 1B). The primary reason given for not allowing same-sex couples to marry is that doing so will lead to undesirable consequences: societal values will be eroded because the government will be committed to sanctioning polygamous marriages. We can now see that the consequences are not expected to follow causally. Same-sex marriages will only 'cause' polygamous marriages in the sense that such marriages will have to be allowed. But the logic by which this would follow is an implicit appeal to the treatment of similar cases in similar ways. Polygamous marriage will follow as a consequence because it is analogous to same-sex marriage and therefore consistency under the law will compel legislators to permit it.

So this is an Appeal to Precedent rather than a Slippery Slope argument. Accordingly, we can ask whether the two cases (same-sex marriage and polygamous marriage) are analogous. What reasons do we have for believing so? And are there relevant dissimilarities that would prevent the precedent from being set?

The arguer in Case 10C actually provides no similarities between the two analogues. Imaginatively, we could propose that both types of case will involve people in an emotionally committed relationship and who have entered into an arrangement of mutual economic dependence. These would seem to be relevant similarities in allowing people to marry. But in this case, it is the dissimilarities that prevent the conclusion from following as the arguer wishes and create the fallacious reasoning. Prior to the enabling legislation, marriage was only available to heterosexual couples.

No relevant difference was seen between these and same-sex couples who were seeking marriage other than their sex. Since it was a principle of the Charter of Rights and Freedoms not to discriminate on the basis of sex, this removed the relevant difference under the law. Fairness demanded that marriage be extended to include same-sex couples. But polygamous relationships are dissimilar in just this way: polygamous groups are not recognized as historically disadvantaged and needing to be protected, and number is not like sex. Number introduces a complexity to the emotional relationship and to the economic arrangements that make these unlike the relevant cases. A range of legal rights are enjoyed by married couples on the basis of their being couples. Extending the number of those involved would change matters to require considerable further legislation. Perhaps this could in time occur, but it would not do so on the basis of the setting of a precedent in the same-sex case. It would have to be argued on different terms.

Critical Questions

Because the Appeal to Precedent is grounded in analogical reasoning, an assessment of these arguments will draw on the general Critical Questions we used to determine the presence of False Analogies. But we also need to include questions that help us identify the specific kind of analogical reasoning involved.

1. Does the argument suggest that an action or proposal will commit us to treating other cases the same and thereby lead to an undesirable consequence?
2. Is the implicit (or explicit) appeal to consistency supported by a good analogical argument?

The Appeal to Precedent is more than just an Argument from Analogy at heart; it is also an argument to a certain consequence. This is what distinguishes it from a more straightforward inductive analogical argument. Our first critical question seeks to detect this

feature of the reasoning. But we also need to distinguish it from
the other argument to consequence that we saw in the previous
chapter, the Slippery Slope, and so we must include the identity
feature that the cases involved are related through likeness rather
than related causally.

The second Critical Question draws us back to the way we evaluate analogical reasoning to determine whether there is a False
Analogy involved, making the argument a fallacious Appeal to
Precedent. But notice that the reasoning here, unlike that in basic
analogical arguments, involves an appeal to an underlying principle of consistency or fairness. This illustrates the kinds of domain
in which arguments of this type are likely to arise. Insofar as consistency is an important value in moral and legal reasoning, avoiding
inconsistency will be an important strategy that adds persuasive-
ness to the reasoning.

This observation also suggests ways fallacies in analogical reasoning of this type may arise. When we speak of principles and
values we are speaking about things that people hold particularly
dear and will go to great lengths to defend in argument. As we
have seen in earlier chapters, such close associations can lead to
ill-considered reasoning and cause people to overlook features of
context that, once identified, may serve to undermine their case.
The failure to think through the dissimilarities between analogues
in an Argument from Analogy may be so common because of this.

4 Two Wrongs by Analogy

Another type of argument that is essentially analogical and quite
controversial is what we call the Two Wrongs by Analogy argument. A short case will illustrate it.

Case 10D
After Janet Jackson's breast was exposed during the halftime show
of the 2004 Superbowl, commentators offered both criticism and

defenses of her actions and the broadcaster that conveyed them. Typical of some of the defenders' arguments is the following:

I don't see quite what all the fuss is about. As bad as the brief bit of nudity during the halftime show might be, it pales beside the gore and violence regularly served up by the networks during prime time viewing.

Unlike the Appeal to Precedent, which may be neutral on the action or proposal that is being considered, the analogy in this type of Two Wrongs by Analogy argument accepts that an action is wrong but argues that it is less wrong than some other action to which it is analogous. We see this in Case 10D, in which the exposure of Janet Jackson's breast is defended as being less wrong than other things that are being shown on television during similar hours. The problem with this argument is that it seems to fall foul of the schoolyard cliché we all remember that "Two wrongs do not make a right." But crucially here the fallacy lies in the analogical reasoning.[9] There may well be other shows that involve offensive or adult material. But what was essential about the Jackson episode was that it was unexpected. Families who might have chosen not to view it had they had advance warning were given no option. By contrast, shows with violence and gore are usually identified as such and parents can decide whether they and their children will view it. This is a major dissimilarity that undermines the analogy.

This is to suggest that Two Wrongs by Analogy arguments that pass the requirements of good analogical reasoning *might* be generally acceptable. In spite of the belief that two wrongs never make a right, some people argue that in certain circumstances responding to one wrong with another is a reasonable course of action. For example, when one country violates a trade agreement and

---

[9] There is a more general kind of 'Two Wrongs' argument that tries to justify a wrong action on the grounds that it attempts to respond to or mitigate a worse wrong. But there is no analogy between the wrongs in this general case.

introduces illegal tariffs on goods from another country, that second country may respond by introducing a similar violation and justify its action on the grounds that the best way to address the first wrong is to introduce an analogous wrong. Clearly, there is no such justification provided in Case 10D, but it helps us consider how we will deal with similar types of arguments. Several Critical Questions will aid our decision making.

Critical Questions

1. Is the wrong that is being justified really analogous to another wrong that has been allowed? That is, does the analogy in the argument meet the Critical Questions for the Argument from Analogy?
2. Is this a case in which fairness of treatment of analogous cases would outweigh our concerns about the wrong's being justified?

These questions clearly take us deeper into the wrongness and rightness of contextual features. In general, our investigation of fallaciousness has become more complex as we have explored arguments with these social and moral ramifications. Clearly, some errors of reasoning have greater import than others, and part of our assessment of such reasoning is to help us think through examples that carry serious moral weight. Fallacy theory will not tell us what is right or wrong in every case, but it will open up the case for us and allow us to explore issues by asking the right kinds of question. We see this here with the second Critical Question. While the first question draws on the concerns over False Analogy that we have already explored, the second question addresses the deeper issue of consistency and fairness that often underlies the choice to employ analogical reasoning. In a case like that of Two Wrongs by Analogy, in which fairness is being appealed to, we must weigh the value of fairness against the concern over the wrong that is being proposed or justified. This will require a different kind of argument and eventual assessment from us, one that takes us beyond the interests of this book into the domain of moral argumentation. But deciding whether a fallacy has been committed is a first step before deciding among the competing values being argued in a piece of reasoning.

CHAPTER EXERCISES

Assess the analogy-based arguments in the following for fallaciousness, using the Critical Questions of this chapter to direct your assessments. In the case of False Analogy, indicate whether the analogies involved are inductive or a priori. Not every piece may involve fallacious reasoning or have identity conditions that fit the schemes of this chapter.

1. Many jurisdictions have mandatory seatbelt legislation, which some people view as an unacceptable restriction on individual liberty, giving rise to arguments like the following:

   To argue that wearing a seatbelt should be law because it is safer than not wearing one is no different than to argue that if a certain style of hat reduces the chance of sunburn on fair days, then everyone, by law, should be forced to wear that style of hat, whenever she goes outdoors. This is an issue of civil liberty and we, like obedient, dull-witted sheep, have allowed this law to stand.

2. The following is a public announcement distributed by motion picture studios. Each statement is accompanied by video images of the actions described.

   You wouldn't steal a car.
   You wouldn't steal a handbag.
   You wouldn't steal a television.
   You wouldn't steal a DVD.

Downloading pirated films is stealing.
Stealing is against the law.
Piracy is a crime.
I: Illegal downloading: Inappropriate for all ages.

3. After the U.S. Supreme Court lifted a ban on gay sex in Texas, the following was reported in *The Guardian*, June 27, 2003. In your evaluation, focus on the claim from the Republican senator.

The US Supreme Court yesterday overturned a Texan law banning sodomy between two men, in a landmark decision that gay rights advocates claimed was a "turning point" in American attitudes toward homosexuality.

The six-to-three verdict carries profound implications for gay rights in the U.S., effectively revoking anti-sodomy laws that exist in 13 states. Legal experts said the ruling also carries wider implications for the right to privacy.

In comments ahead of the judgment, the republican senator Rick Santorum had stirred controversy when he said that if sodomy were legalised "then you have the right to bigamy, you have the right to polygamy, you have the right to incest, you have the right to adultery, you have the right to anything."

4. The following is from a letter to the *Chicago Tribune*, July 16, 2004, accessed July 16, 2004, http://www.chicagotribune.com/news/opinion/letters/chi-0407160271jul16,1,5599338.story?coll=ch-newsopinionvoice-hed:

Never in the history of human civilization has prohibition curbed the use of mind-altering substances. Human beings by nature look beyond their present reality.

There was a time when Christopher Columbus was thought a crackpot for proposing that the world was round. Galileo nearly got lynched for proposing the revolutionary thought that the Earth revolved around the sun. It's long past time for civilized nations to realize that, just as these "revolutionary" theories proved to be dead-on accurate, the prohibition of marijuana, cocaine and heroin will not only prove to be bad law but will never stop people from seeking them.

Until and unless drug use is considered a health issue instead of a law-enforcement issue, prisons will be filled by users and funded by the rest of us. But the big three of the illegal drugs – which collectively kill fewer people in a year than tobacco kills in any given week – are opposed on lawmaking floors by the big-money killers: the alcohol and tobacco lobbies, the prison builders and the pharmaceutical companies.

The hypocrisy is obscene.

5. From the *New York Times*, July 22, 2004, accessed July 23, 2004, http://www.nytimes.com/2004/07/23/opinion/l23abortion.html:

Barbara Ehrenreich's defense of abortion begs the question. Abortion is legal, but so was racism under apartheid and killing Jews under the Nazis. The question is whether abortion is good or evil, and the growing consensus in America is that despite its standing under the law, abortion is a repulsive evil, especially partial-birth abortion.

6. The following letter appeared in the *Boston Globe*, July 8, 2004, accessed July 8, 2004, http://www.boston.com/news/globe/editorial_opinion/letters/articles/2004/07/08/growing_up_with_a_father/:

I agree with Joan Vennochi that the declining values and standards of our nation's youth, illustrated and reinforced by the pervasive negative themes in hip-hop and rap music, are not limited to any single group in our society ("Cosby's comments cut deep," op ed, July 6). Rather, they cut across racial and socioeconomic boundaries. She concludes by saying we all should contemplate why this is so, and, more important, what is the solution.

I am reminded of an event that occurred in Africa several years ago involving the relocation of an elephant herd from one area where they had come into conflict with humans to another that had been set aside as a nature reserve.

The relocation specialists decided it was too difficult to relocate the large adult males and chose to euthanize them instead. After that, the relocation went as planned. A few years later, park officials were stymied by the widespread killing of a rare breed of rhinoceros in the park. Initially, the deaths were blamed on poachers, but later they realized that it was actually the juvenile male elephants that were responsible. When they added older adult males to the herd as role models for the juvenile males, the killing immediately stopped.

In our own society, it is reported that 70 percent of kids in urban America go to bed without a dad in their home. According to the National Fatherhood Initiative, children who live with their fathers are less likely to be poor; use drugs; experience educational, health, emotional and behavioral problems; be victims of child abuse; or engage in criminal behavior than those who live absent their biological fathers.

Without fathers or other adult male role models, our kids will continue to look to the culture, friends, and/or celebrities to fill the void. MTV doesn't offer too much in the way of positive influence. Fatherhood is not only important, it is critical. It is a bit ironic that a man who wrote a book on it didn't point this out.

7. A letter to the *Daily Telegraph*, May 23, 2004, accessed May 24, 2004, http://www.telegraph.co.uk/opinion/main.jhtml;sessionid= ZRNSVALRGHXM3QFIQMGSM5WAVC-BQWJVC?xml=/opinion/ 2004/05/23/do2301.xml&sSheet=/opinion/2004/05/23/ixop.html &secureRefresh=true&_requestid=21564:

I am sure that most people would side with the Israeli court, and insist that the possibility of preventing say 10 deaths would not justify the introduction of torture. But what if torturing a single individual prevented 1,000 or 10,000 or 100,000 deaths? At some point, it becomes morally impossible to maintain that an individual's right not to be tortured is so important that it outweighs the certain murder of thousands of others. Torture then stops being the "absolute evil" which the convention says it is. It becomes an evil which sometimes is capable of being the lesser of two abominations – and one which it can be right to choose.

8. The following letter is from a retired marine sergeant to the *Washington Post* forum, June 16, 2004, accessed June 19, 2004,

http://forums.washingtonpost.com/wpeditorials/messages/?msg=
3530.1:

Situation.
　You, your spouse and children were on a plane taxiing to take-off.
The plane was ordered back to the terminal and a bomb was found
aboard.
　Question.
　Would you or your spouse be concerned about the interrogation
methods used to obtain the information which found the bomb?
　How many American and Iraqi lives were saved because of infor-
mation obtained from prisoners at Abu Ghraib?
　Suppose that was the source of information concerning the bomb
found on your plane? Would you declare the information "inadmiss-
able" and ask that the pilot continue with the flight?

9. The following is part of a response to an earlier piece in *New
   Internationalist*, June 24, 2004, accessed July 1, 2004, http://www.
   newint.org/feedback/index.htm:

I am compelled to respond to the constant barrage of anti war
rhetoric from the NI and other similar publications. I want to
remind you that Winston Churchill had no conclusive evidence that
Hitler was mounting a war machine as early as 1933 nor was there
any conclusive evidence of Concentration Camps either, nor did
that Famous League of Nations (now the UN) or the Allies have
any mandate to interfere in Spain when it blew up under Hitler's
sponsorship. I suppose that Saddam is just working on Chemo Ther-
apy equipment to ease the suffering of his people. The $25000
bonus paid to suicide terrorists in Israel preceding the feeding of
his own people is not evidence of support for terrorism, not to
mention Abu Nidal's now evicted residence in Baghdad. Abu Nidal
murdered people in Munich, Vienna, Milan and Frankfurt, ok not
entirely indiscriminately, they were Israelis, Jews or just standing
close to the EL AL ticket counter, which makes them Zionist Imperi-
alists to be exterminated. . . . I do not advocate war but sometimes it is
necessary, as it was in WWII, there too a lot of innocent Germans died
in Dresden and Berlin, not to mention Hiroshima and Nagasaki.

10. In September 2005, the Ontario government seriously considered adopting Islam's Sharia tribunals as part of the family law system (it subsequently decided against doing so). The proposal ignited a fierce debate between supporters and opponents. The following is from a latter to the *National Post*, September 9, 2005:

> The promoters of Sharia law are not suggesting that the whole of Canada be turned into a religious state. But what they are suggesting is that – insofar as their parishioners are concerned – the secular state will return to the religious state. Only a small beginning. Only a small wedge. But wedges get bigger. By what logic can we presume that other religious and non religious organizations will not see their organizations deserving of the same consideration?... The ramifications that this undertaking will have on the whole of our free society should be of grave concern for us all.

FURTHER READING

While there is a wide use of analogical argument in academic literature, less attention is paid to the problems of such arguments, and their associated fallacies. The best current work available for those who want to begin looking further into this issue are two chapters in the work of Trudy Govier, Chapter 9 in *The Philosophy of Argument* (Newport News, VA: Vales Press, 1999), and Chapter 4 in *Problems in Argument Analysis and Evaluation* (Dordrecht: Foris, 1987).

Index

abortion, 29
Accent, Fallacy of, 7, 9, 57, 58
Accident, Fallacy of, 7
ad baculum, 104, 108–113
  Critical Questions for, 112–113
ad hominem argument, 12, 13, 81–97,
    105, 117
  abusive, 92–93
  circumstantial, 93–94
  Critical Questions for, 89–91
  defined, 86
  fallacious form, 86
  general problems, 88–89
  Guilt by Association, 96–97
  Locke's definition, 82
  tu quoque, 94–96
ad ignorantiam, 14, 104, 105, 117–121
  Critical Questions for, 120–121
ad misericordiam, 104, 105, 113–116
  Critical Questions for, 115–116
ad populum, 14, 104, 105–108, 130
  Critical Questions for, 107–108
ad verecundiam, 12, 84, 104, 127–144
  Critical Questions for, 135–143
    bias, 140–141
    consensus, 141–142
    consequences, 142–143
    field, 137–138
    identity, 136–137
    relevance, 138–139
    testability, 139–140
  see also Appeal to Authority

Affirming the Consequent, 53
  fallacy of, 43, 50, 62
ambiguity, 58, 67
Amphiboly, 7, 8, 57, 58–60
analogical reasoning, 33, 188
  see also Argument from Analogy
analogy, defined, 194
Appeal to Authority
  argument *of* authority, 129
  Critical Questions for general appeal,
    133–134
  modern appeals defined, 129
    see also ad verecundiam
Appeal to Experts, 131
  see also Appeal to Authority
Appeal to Force, *see ad baculum*
Appeal to Ignorance, *see ad
  ignorantiam*
Appeal to Pity, *see ad misericordiam*
Appeal to Popularity, *see ad populum*
Appeal to Precedent, 5, 188–189,
    201–205, 206
  Critical Questions for fallacious
    appeals, 204–205
  fallacious type, 200–201, 205
Argument from Analogy, 194–195, 197,
    200–201, 204, 205
  a priori type, 196, 199
    defined, 196
  inductive type, 196, 197, 201, 202
    defined, 196
  see also analogical reasoning

Argument from Consequences,
    183–184, 205
  Critical Questions for, 184
  fallacy of, 184
Argument from Correlation to Cause,
    173
Argument from Ignorance, *see ad*
    ignorantiam
Argument from Signs, 53
arguments
  ethotic, 81
  intention behind, 1
  schemes, 16
  social character, 43
  strength of, 1–6
  structure of, 1
  see also individual arguments
Aristotelian tradition of fallacy, 2, 8,
    16, 34, 57
Aristotle, 7, 9, 16, 19, 42, 50, 53, 59,
    69, 82, 85, 113, 129
  on cause, 175
  Prior Analytics, 6, 45
  Rhetoric, 6, 8, 81, 174
  role in the history of fallacy, 6–8,
    129
  Sophistical Refutations, 6, 7, 15, 16,
    50, 58, 73, 82, 175
  syllogism, 44–49
  Topics, 73–75

Beevor, Antony, 181
Begging the Question, 7, 9
  Critical Questions for, 76–77
Biased Statistics, Fallacy of, 161–163,
    166
biases, 140, 157–158, 159
  vested interests, 141
Blair, J. Anthony, 65, 66
Bono, 133
Brinton, Alan, 86
burden of proof, 5, 14, 71, 91, 93, 107,
    134, 178, 201
Bush, George W., 111

causal hypothesis, 174, 178
causal reasoning (or argument), 173,
    174, 179, 201
  Critical Questions for, 181–183
circular reasoning, 72, 75
  see also Begging the Question
Combinations of Words, 7, 57

distinguished from fallacy of
    composition, 58
Complex Question, 30, 69–72
  Critical Questions for, 71–72
Consequent, Fallacy of, 7
context, 23, 25, 121, 155, 176, 178, 183,
    207
  in the relation between formal and
    informal fallacies, 52
Copi, I., 34
correlation, 173, 174, 178, 180
critical discussion, 22, 64
Critical Questions (for evaluation),
    13–14, 26–28, 32–33, 51–52,
    60–62, 69, 71–72, 76–77, 89–91,
    107–108, 112–113, 115–116,
    120–121, 133–134, 135–143, 156,
    166–167, 181–183, 184, 187–188,
    196, 204–205, 207–208

Däniken, Erich von, 138
Darwin, Charles, 21–22, 23, 141
deception, 15, 17
deduction
  rules for syllogisms, 45–46
  validity, 17, 42
Denying the Antecedent, Fallacy of, 49
Denying the Consequent, 42, 43, 117
dialectical debate, 76
  arguments, 9
  and the concept of fallacy, 8
Distribution, Fallacies of, 45–49
Division of Words, 7, 57
  distinguished from fallacy of
    division, 58

Eemeren, Frans H. van, 10, 64, 90, 110,
    195
Equivocation, 7, 53, 57, 58, 59–60, 67
  Critical Questions for, 60–62
ethotic reasoning, 85
  defined, 81

fallacy
  as argument, 9
  definition, 1–2, 6, 9, 12, 15, 16, 17
  dialectical shift, 10, 77, 90
  formal fallacies, 43–54
    Critical Questions for, 51–52
  informal fallacies, 43, 52
  psychological phenomenon, 9, 75
  standard treatment, 9

and validity, 2, 9–10
see also sophistical refutations
False Analogy
Critical Questions for, 196, 204, 207
Fallacy of, 195, 196–201, 205
figure of speech, *see* Form of
Expression
Form of Expression, Fallacy of, 7, 57,
58
Four Terms, Fallacy of, 53
Freud, Sigmund, 141

Gambler's Fallacy, 156
generalizations, 150–167, 195
absolute or universal, 150–151
inductive, 151, 158
presumptive, defeasible, 151–152,
153, 156–158
sweeping, 154. *see also secundum
quid*
see also Hasty Generalization
Govier, Trudy, 94, 195, 196
Grice, Paul, 33, 36, 130
Grootendorst, Rob, 10, 64, 90, 110,
195
Guilt by Association, 4, 13, 96–97, 141
see also ad hominem argument

Hamblin, C. L., 2, 9, 11, 14, 19, 42, 43,
46, 48, 76, 82, 104, 131, 152, 153,
195
basic treatment of fallacy, 9–10
Hansen, Hans V., 11
Hasty Generalization, 150, 154, 158,
159
Critical Questions for, 156
heuristics of judgment, 156–158, 176
Houellebecq, Michel, case of, 175–176
Huxley, Julian, 194

ignoratio elenchi, 7, 34, 41, 62
defined, 34
see also Irrelevant Conclusion
Illicit Major, Fallacy of, 48
Illicit Minor, Fallacy of, 48
induction, 149
arguments, 54, 163, 167
validity, 17
Insufficient Statistics, Fallacy of,
159–160, 166
invalidity, 41, 44
invasion of Iraq, 29

irrelevance, 23, 31, 33
see also relevance
Irrelevant Conclusion, 34–36
defined, 34
*see also ignoratio elenchi; non
sequitur*

Jackson, Janet, 205–206
Johnson, Ralph H., 65, 66

Kahneman, Daniel, 156–157, 165, 176
Kantianism, 198

Locke, John, 82, 93, 104, 117, 128–129,
132, 143
Lomborg affair, 2–4, 83–84, 96–97

Many Questions, Fallacy of, 7, 9, 69
Massey, Gerald, 43
measurement error, *see* opinion polls
Mill, John Stuart, 76
Misidentified Cause, 174
Fallacy of, 179
see also causal reasoning: Critical
Questions for
moral argumentation, role of fallacy
theory in, 207–208

necessary condition, defined, 51
Negativity, Fallacy of, 48
Noncause, Fallacy of, 7
non sequitur, 34–36
see also Irrelevant Conclusion

opinion polls, 149, 159–167
Critical Questions for, 166–167
margin of error, 166
measurement error, 163–166
sampling error, 162
Orwell, George, 65–66
out of body experiences (OBEs), 140,
143

petitio principii, 9, 72
see also Begging the Question
Pinto, Robert C., 174, 176
Plato, 7
Academy, 7
Apology, 95
Dialogues, 195
Euthydemus, 59
Port Royal Logic, 149, 152

post hoc reasoning, 174
  Fallacy of, 174–179
  two types explained, 174
  see also causal reasoning: Critical
    Questions for
Powers, Lawrence, 62
pragma-dialectics
  rules, 64, 87, 110
  theory of fallacy, 10
  treatment of the *ad hominem*, 87–88
Principle of Charity, 31, 35, 67, 177
  example of, 153

random selection of samples, 163
Red Herring, 28–33
  distinguished from the Straw Man,
    28
relevance, 23–25, 29, 33, 36, 91,
    138–139, 198
  in analogical arguments, 198, 199,
    203
  dialectical relevance, 24
  probative relevance, 23
  see also irrelevance
representative sample, 149, 159
rhetorical argument, 53

Salmon, Wesley, 11, 132
same-sex marriage debate, 4–5
sampling error, *see* opinion polls
seal hunt, 28
secundum quid, 7, 150, 155, 158
Slippery Slope reasoning, 5
  Critical Questions for, 187–188
  defined, 185
  distinguished from Appeal to
    Precedent, 189, 201, 202, 203, 205
  Fallacy of, 189

Socrates, 7, 95
sophistical refutations, 7–8
  that depend on language, 7, 57
  that do not depend on language, 7
sophists, 7
Spock, (Dr.) Benjamin, 139
Straw Man (or Person), 12, 19–28, 31,
    33, 41, 60
  Critical Questions for evaluation,
    26–28
sufficient condition, defined, 51

testimony, 130, 136
Thomson, Judith, 196
tu quoque arguments
  see ad hominem arguments
Tversky, Amos, 156–157, 165, 176
Two Wrongs by Analogy
  Critical Questions for evaluation,
    207–208
  defined, 206
  distinguished from general Two
    Wrongs argument, 206
  Fallacy of, 205–208

Undistributed Middle, fallacy of, 47
utilitarianism, 198

Vagueness, 166, 167
  Critical Questions for, 67–69
  Fallacy of, 9, 64–69

Walton, Douglas, 13, 43, 51, 74, 150,
    151, 153, 154, 184
Whately, Richard, 14
Willard, Charles, 143
Wisdom, John, 196
Woods, John, 74

Printed in the United States
By Bookmasters